New Tole & Folk Art Designs

New

Tole

& Folk Art

Designs

PAINTING TECHNIQUES AND PATTERNS

Joyce Howard

Chilton Book Company
Radnor, Pennsylvania

Copyright © 1979 by Joyce Howard

Published in Radnor, Pennsylvania, by Chilton Book Company
and simultaneously in Don Mills, Ontario, Canada,
by Thomas Nelson & Sons, Ltd.
Manufactured in the United States of America

Illustrations by the author
Photographs by Reed Andariese and Leigh Lydecker
Designed by Arlene Putterman

Library of Congress Cataloging in Publication Data
Howard, Joyce.
    New tole and folk art designs.
    1. Tole painting.   2. Design, Decorative.
3. Folk art.   I. Title.
TT385.H68   745.7'2   79-11582
ISBN 0-8019-6821-6
ISBN 0-8019-6822-4 pbk.

1 2 3 4 5 6 7 8 9 0   8 7 6 5 4 3 2 1 0 9

*Dedicated with love to Doris Henry,
my Mother, whose early encouragement
and persistence opened the door to
the world of art.*

Contents ～❂

Contents

New Tole & Folk Art Designs

1

Welcome to Folk Art Painting

Welcome to the world of decorative tole and folk art painting. Here, skilled craftspeople carry on a tradition that reflects centuries of beautiful design work. Successive generations have borrowed the ethnic motifs, bold symbols, and figurative art from artists before them, creating their own folk art. This book offers new ideas, painting techniques, and patterns to help you become the artist.

Two methods of decorative painting are taught in this book: the new acrylic and mud method, and the ever-popular tole painting with oils. A large collection of patterns is provided for you to use or adapt, and you will learn how to compose your own designs as well. We will also discuss how to get both old and new items ready for decorative painting, and how to paint on materials other than metal and wood.

The origins of folk art painting

Unlike most other art forms, decorative folk art painting has its roots among the common people. The simple designs and motifs echo the lifestyles and attitudes of particular regions. Many date back to the early Middle Ages. Even the term tole painting has a regional basis. *Tôle* means tin in French, and originally the French painted designs on tinware. Painted furniture was the hallmark of a region extend-

[1]

ing from Scandinavia to the middle Rhine, Switzerland, Romania and western Russia, while western England, northern Germany and the Mediterranean countries were known for their ornamental wood carvings and appliqués.

In Alpine and lower Germany, the ceilings of medieval village churches and rural castles were often painted with historical and religious themes. These decorative ceilings influenced the development of furniture painting and spawned the growth of a circle of peasant imitators. Stencils on late Gothic cupboards are examples of this. Late medieval chests in Hungary and Romania were greatly influenced by the paintings of the Renaissance and Baroque cabinetmakers.

A new type of furniture painting was popular in Norway during the eighteenth and nineteenth centuries. Rosemahling, the freehand painting of colorful flowers, took the place of stencil art. Today, rosemahling (mahling means painting in Norwegian) is a favorite decorative technique.

Color preferences also developed regionally. Black was often used in upper Austria; glowing vermillion and light blue with orange were used in Norway; and strong yellows and greens were popular in Germany.

The craft tradition was brought to America (New England and Pennsylvania in particular) during the eighteenth and nineteenth centuries. Many sources were used as inspiration for the new decorative painters: textiles, wallpaper, pottery, porcelain, carved furniture, and woodwork. The characteristics of the designs were different in each region. For example, tulips were much wider and bolder in Pennsylvania than in New England. Also, most folk painting in Pennsylvania had a geometric, overlapping design, while New England designs had a more delicate touch and a more realistic quality.

Bolder and simpler colors were used in American folk art. Painters mixed their own colors, so they were restricted to what they could readily make themselves. Native yellow and red clays were commonly used to make paint. Vegetable dyes, crushed berries, shrubs and herbs were used for green—skunk cabbage was the choice of the day. Browns and dull yellows were extracted from the bark of trees, and the indigo plant supplied the color blue. Indigo was scarce, as it had to be imported from India.

With a style of its own, American folk painting became very popular. By the late 1800s, it was in great demand. The wealthy began acquiring the finer pieces, and what was once a simple, colorful expression to brighten a plain lifestyle became a valuable art object. Today museums and private collections preserve many examples of this treasured craft.

The art of fractur

The word "fractur" is rarely used in the everyday discussion of folk art. Fractur is an illuminated writing, prevalent in Pennsylvania during the eighteenth and nineteenth centuries, in which the lettering is done in the Gothic German style called *Fraktur-Schriften*. Fractur is basically a quill pen and watercolor technique adapted from the European art of manuscript illumination.

In America fractur developed into a very distinctive art. Early fractur was religious in character. Examples are prayer and hymn book illustrations. Later came ornamental documents such as birth, baptismal and death certificates, family registers, Valentines, music books, bookplates, and presentation pieces. A contemporary example of fractur is shown in figure 1-1.

William Penn (1644–1718) did much to encourage the art of fractur in America. The earliest known work dates from 1728 and was done by the religious members of the Ephrata Cloister in the town of Ephrata in Lancaster County. The art continued to flourish for two centuries, though it had practically disappeared in Europe. Schoolmasters and clergy accomplished in the art earned extra money working a fractur on documents needed by the colonists. By 1819, the art was very much in vogue, and it was then that Johann Krauss put together an instruction book so school children could be taught the art from a fractur alphabet.

The lettering in fractur was done with a goose quill pen and the illustrations outlined with a mixture of india ink and sepia to create an earthy color. The illustrations were then painted with watercolors of light hues. The illustrations on some manuscripts were given a slight sheen by using special caked colors. These colors were liquefied with whiskey and cherry gum varnish diluted with water. The dyes were

[3]

Fig. 1–1. *A contemporary example of fractur.*

made from old recipes handed down through the generations. Colors were blood red, soft greens, golden yellows, and delicate shades of blue.

Fractur designs were derived originally from German folk art, but American designs such as eagles joined forces with the traditional designs. Symbolism lay behind many of the popular motifs. In Germany, the tulip was known as the holy lily, its three petals representing the Trinity. Mermaids symbolized the dual nature of Christ, half man, half diety. The heart symbolized love and marriage, and unicorns represented virginity. The lion, crown, and unicorn were old heraldic symbols. Fractur is an important link to other Pennsylvania folk art. Many of the patterns found on barns, furniture, and utensils were adapted from fractur designs.

It is interesting to note how the style of fractur changed. On American soil it gradually developed a more primitive character. Design and color became much brighter and stronger. It was a fresher and freer approach compared to the soft hues and delicate work of the earlier manuscripts.

Pennsylvania fractur is an unsurpassed example of our rural art tradition. The early fracturs have become very important to collectors and can be seen in several museums throughout the country, especially Bucks and Lancaster counties in Pennsylvania.

Fractur has had a continuing influence in our lives. Every day we can see a familiar motif or the decorative Gothic lettering in some form of advertisement or publication. Interior decorators have used color combinations and fabrics with designs emulating early fractur art. Paintings used today as decorative touches for homes are often patterned after early pieces of fractur. You may have pottery or china in your home that was greatly influenced by fractur. Look at the designs used to decorate many trays and placemats today. As you begin your own painting, keep in mind the wealth of ideas that can be had from this early style.

2

Selecting and Preparing Decorative Objects

Finding objects to decorate with folk art painting can be an adventure in itself. You'll want to collect wooden and tin boxes, plaques, mirrors, tinware of interesting shapes, and furniture. Many plaques, sconces and mirrors can be purchased in craft shops, but garage sales, secondhand shops, and junk and antique stores are much more fun to prowl through.

Together with friends, plan trips throughout areas such as Pennsylvania, Vermont, New Hampshire and Massachusetts. Southern states also have many exciting junk and antique stores to visit. To shop successfully, take back roads off the beaten paths. You will discover shops with prices much lower than those in major cities. Goodies such as old coffee grinders, seed planters, nail kegs, milk cans, trays, bowls, buckets, etc., will make your searches worthwhile.

Preparing the surface

It's a good idea to collect several different pieces for future painting sessions. Set aside a week or so to prepare several pieces for decorating so that when the artistic mood befalls you, you can simply select a ready-to-paint object and go directly to the exciting part of designing and decorating.

OLD WOOD

At times, you may wish to use the painted surface of an old wooden piece as the base coat for your decorative painting. This is possible only if the paint is in very good condition. Check it carefully for cracking and peeling. If these are present, remove the paint. If you paint and varnish over old paint that is in poor condition, the old paint will continue to crack, and all your decorating efforts will be wasted. If the paint is in good condition, sand it lightly with 0000 steel wool before painting.

Any varnished surface must be stripped. Once the varnish is removed, an existing stain may be left exposed as the background for your design. If you want to conceal the stain entirely and paint the whole piece, you must seal the surface with an opaque pigmented shellac to prevent the stain from bleeding through the paint. Pigmented shellac is a white, opaque sealer; do not use clear or orange shellac.

Stripping and preparing an old wood surface is illustrated in figure 2-1. Many newer paint and varnish removers, such as Zip Strip or Stripease, have a thick consistency that is easy to apply as there is less dripping. Always follow the directions on the can. Many strippers soften the finish so that it can be removed with a scrub brush or rag. Allow the remover enough time to work, and apply it several times if

Fig. 2–1. Preparing old wood surface. Left: Thoroughly remove finish with paint and varnish remover, then neutralize with denatured alcohol, and sand and steel wool lightly. Center: Apply two coats of base paint; let paint dry completely between coats. Right: Paint design after base coat is dry.

OLD WOOD

necessary. If you must use a paint scraper to remove the old paint, be careful not to gouge the wood.

When the wood is thoroughly clean, it can be neutralized by wiping it down with Carbona (a cleaning fluid) or denatured alcohol. Let it dry, then smooth it with fine sandpaper and 0000 steel wool. Fill any holes with plastic wood, let dry, and sand smooth again.

The above procedure is preferred to the commercial stripping vats where furniture is dipped into acid solution. This solution is detrimental because it depletes the wood of its oil and raises the grain. A little extra labor is always worth the effort to produce a fine piece of furniture that has years of lasting quality.

Your wood is now ready for the base coat. Work carefully—if it is not applied correctly, ridges can build up, and your work will not look professional. The paint you use doesn't have to be oil base; latex or acrylic low-lustre paints are easier to clean up. (Do not use flat or high-gloss latex—be sure it is semi-gloss.) If using these water-based paints, use a 2- or 3-inch nylon brush and paint with broad, even strokes. Check for paint build-up and smooth lightly with the brush. Allow your work to dry for 24 hours before applying a second coat for good coverage protection.

NEW WOOD

The most important step in preparing new wood is to provide a smooth, clean surface (figure 2-2). Sand all edges and surfaces with at least two grades of sandpaper, finishing with fine or very fine paper.

Fig. 2–2. Preparing new wood surface. Left: Finish with fine sandpaper and remove particles with tack cloth. Center: Apply two coats of base paint, sanding lightly between coats. Right: Paint design over dry base coat.

NEW WOOD

[8]

Always sand with the grain, using a light, even pressure. Before painting the base coat, clean all the sanding dust from the wood—a tack cloth, available at paint stores and craft shops, does a thorough job.

For easy cleanup, use latex or acrylic low-lustre paint (not flat or high-gloss) for the base coat. Be sure to paint both sides of a plaque to prevent warping, and always use two coats on all your pieces. Water-based paints may raise the grain slightly, so sand lightly with 0000 steel wool between coats to insure a smooth finish. Allow 24 hours between coats.

METAL

Metal requires even more careful preparation than wood, because rust is always a threat. If you are reusing an old metal object, you must remove all rust and prevent any new rust from forming (figure 2-3). Sand loose rust with rough sandpaper, and use naval jelly or muriatic acid for stubborn rust and pitted marks. Be sure to follow instructions on the bottle and wear rubber gloves—many of these chemicals can burn the skin. After the rust has been thoroughly removed, wash the

Fig. 2–3. *Preparing metal surface. Left: Remove rust, and clean metal with vinegar and water solution. Center: Paint with rust-inhibiting primer and let dry completely. Right: Apply two coats of base paint.*

METAL

[9]

metal with equal parts of vinegar and water to neutralize and lift any oil or chemical traces from the metal. If you use a new, rust-free metal object, washing with vinegar and water is the first step in preparing the surface.

Allow the cleaned metal to dry completely, and paint it with a rust-inhibiting primer. The primer should dry for two or three days before you apply the colored base coat. Oil or low-lustre water-based (acrylic or latex) paint may be used. Apply two coats, and let the first coat dry before applying the second. Wait 24 hours before painting your design.

Cutting your own wood pieces ·

Once you have progressed past the early stages of folk painting, you may discover the joy of designing and cutting your own wood pieces. Even though a supply of varied shapes and sizes of wood may be available, in time most artists feel the urge to try their own hand at cutting wood (figure 2-4). It is not a difficult task, and a little practice will make you an expert.

Choose the variety of wood carefully; each has its own characteristics. I recommend clear pine for most decorative painting because it is soft enough for distressing (gouging the wood to give it an aged look), and it is absorbent enough for the mud stain. If your wood is too hard, you will have difficulty painting it as well as cutting it. Paint will not penetrate the grain, and distressing becomes difficult if not impossible. Also, stains will not wipe off completely, making it difficult to shade your art work. On the other hand, extremely soft wood such as balsam is not recommended. It is too porous and spongy, breaks easily, and cannot withstand the rough handling required for antiquing.

On a piece of paper, design a full-scale pattern of the shape you want to cut. Fold the pattern in half, and cut down the center fold to cut out half the design. Using half of the pattern insures that your wood piece will be symmetrical. Tape the pattern onto the wood and outline it lightly with pencil. Then remove the pattern, flip it over, and carefully align it with the center line you just traced (figure 2-5).

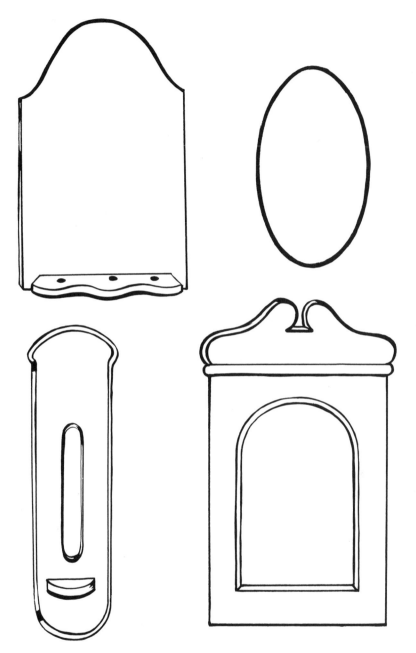

Fig. 2–4. *Typical designs of wooden wall pieces.*

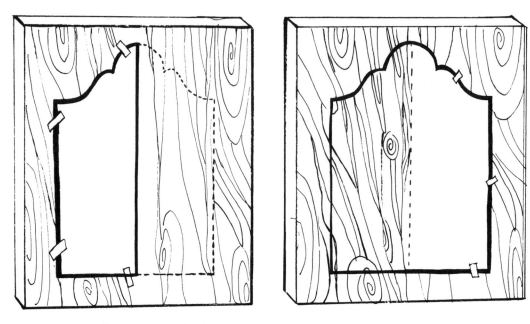

Fig. 2–5. *Use half of the pattern to trace both sides of your design onto the wood.*

Tape the pattern in place and trace it onto the wood. Both sides of your wood piece should now match.

To cut the wood, I recommend a portable electric jigsaw. This tool is also known as a saber saw, and it is perfect for decorative wood-working. The portable jigsaw weighs about 3½ pounds and can be carried easily from job to job. Special blades are made to cut different types of wood, metal or plastic, so be sure to use the recommended blade. Use a straight edge as a guide for cutting straight lines. Press forward and slightly down for a smooth cut.

Once cut, the edges of the wood should be sanded smooth. Decorative edges will enhance the appearance of any wood piece, but such skilled sanding and carving are beyond the abilities of most novices. However, if you have access to a router, the task is simple and very worthwhile. A portable electric router can do in minutes a job requiring hours of skilled hand work. This safe, versatile tool can cut through and into wood at varying depths. Figure 2-6 shows a few of the many shapes different blades can produce. If you plan to design and cut many

RABBET

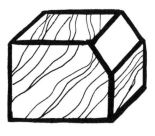

CHAMFER

COVE

Fig. 2–6. Router edges.

of your own decorative wood pieces, you may want to consider investing in a router.

Finally, sand the entire surface lightly to prepare it for painting. A portable electric sander will make this job much easier. Both orbital and belt types work well, although the orbital sanders are more popular. After sanding, the wood is ready for the base coat of paint.

3

Creating
Your Own Designs

Sources for designs

Everyone can be a designer. The first step is to find interesting subjects for your motifs. Chapter 16 provides over 50 original folk art and tole motifs and patterns that can be traced for your folk art file. Keep the file in a large manila envelope marked "Folk Art." These designs will then be at your fingertips whenever you need them. Keeping such a file will save you time in searching endlessly through magazines for ideas.

New designs can be created from parts of old ones. Called cribbing, this method borrows and rearranges designs from several sources to form one new design. Figure 3-1 shows how three separate designs can be cribbed to form a new one. You will be amazed at the new patterns you can create.

Some influential design sources are children's books, books of flower prints, greeting cards, wallpaper, fabrics, tiles, porcelain, magazines, travel posters and carved woodwork. Build your own library of folk art designs and ideas.

A visit to your local library will be quite helpful and rewarding. They willingly allow you to trace from their books, providing you place a sheet of clear, stiff plastic (available in art stores) over the page, place

Fig. 3–1. *The design on the far right has been cribbed from the other three.*

tracing paper over that, and proceed to trace your design. Spend your free afternoons or evenings tracing designs for your folk art file.

Remember to follow the general shape of the object to be decorated when choosing a design, unless you're trying to create an unusual design effect. For instance, if you have a tall, rectangular area on the side of a bureau, be sure the design is tall and not small and horizontal (figure 3-2). For the top of a bureau where a design is needed in the center, choose one that lies horizontally. A round table would naturally have a design that is either central, or one that is used as a border around the edge of the table. After several attempts, your eye will become accustomed to what shapes and designs look best where. Take it slow, and keep painting.

How to compose a simple design

Incorporating patterns is not as difficult as it may seem. Patterns for new designs may be used several times by removing one part and adding another. Make several thumbnail sketches before the final drawing. Fruits and flowers are the simplest form of design for a beginner.

Let's take one example of a pattern in the making (figure 3-3). For balance, plan to have the weight of the design at the bottom. Start with

[15]

Fig. 3–2. The shape of a design should fit the shape of the object it is painted on.

Fig. 3–3. *Building a pattern.*

a decorative vase, and carry the eye vertically with a stem through the center. Add a few leaves at the base of the stem (figure 3-3, top).

As the eye is carried up, begin to add decorative touches such as a heart and a flower on either side (figure 3-3, middle). Bring focus and balance to the top of the design with a large tulip. You are now pulling the design vertically and horizontally (figure 3-3, bottom).

How to enlarge a design

Designs can be enlarged to fit the space you want to decorate. You may also want to enlarge portions of a pattern to form a new design. Figure 3-4 shows the principle of enlarging a pattern by hand. It is also

Fig. 3–4. Enlarging a design. Left: Original traced pattern with grid. Right: Grid drawn to desired size, and pattern copied square by square.

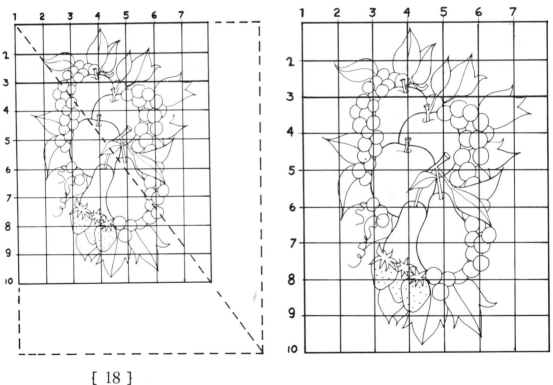

Fig. 3–5.   *Transfer the traced design to the surface using graphite paper and a soft pencil.*

possible to enlarge a design with an enlarging photocopier; check your phone directory for a nearby copy shop.

To enlarge a design by hand, draw a grid over it. (Trace the design first if you don't want to draw directly on it.) If the new design is to be 7 inches wide, divide the width of the original design into seven equal squares. Continue drawing the squares vertically until the design is covered with a grid—be sure to keep the squares of equal size.

Next, on a piece of paper big enough for the enlarged design, draw a grid, 7 inches wide, of 1-inch squares. This grid should have the same number of horizontal and vertical squares as the grid over the original design. Number the squares in each grid to correspond to each other. Now, carefully copy the outline of the design square by square. Be sure to keep the proportions of the outline the same in each square as you copy.

How to transfer a pattern

After the base coat has dried, trace the pattern onto it and decorate.

First trace the pattern onto tracing paper; then tape the paper over the area to be painted. Always use masking tape—cellophane tape strips the paint from the base coat. Slide graphite paper with the shiny side down under the tracing paper. Retrace the design with a sharpened soft pencil (figure 3-5). Remove the tracing paper and graphite paper, and the design is ready to paint.

4

Brushes, Paints and Using Color

Before discussing painting techniques, it is important to become familiar with the tools of painting. The brushes and paints you choose and how you use them will affect the quality of your finished work. Learning to paint is not difficult if you are prepared with the proper tools and motivation.

Brushes

For both acrylic and oil painting, choose only high-quality short-handled, red sable watercolor brushes. Only two brushes are needed for acrylic painting: a short-handled, pointed #5 and a short-handled pointed #2, both in the Grumbacher Beaux Arts Series. For oil paints, you will need the following brushes: #7 large, flat brush; #4 small, flat brush; #5 large, pointed brush; and #2 small, pointed brush.

In choosing a good quality sable brush, flick your finger across the bristles, snapping the hairs. The stronger the brush snaps back, the better the brush. A camel's hair brush is weak and has little resilience. Performance is needed for high quality work, and only the better brush will provide it.

Be sure to clean brushes thoroughly after every use. Clean acrylic brushes in water, oil brushes in turpentine. The slightest amount of paint left in the hairs next to the metal ferrule is the fastest way to ruin a good brush. Hairs will protrude and eventually the point will be lost. Do not leave brushes standing in water, or the bristles will lose their life.

Store brushes in a jar or can, with the bristles pointing up and the handles down. To preserve the shape of a brush used with oil paints, put a slight amount of petroleum jelly on the bristles and shape them with your fingers. To remove the jelly, wash the brush in turpentine. Do not use petroleum jelly to shape brushes used with acrylics as it is not water soluble.

When you are ready to store your acrylic brushes, clean them with a mild facial soap and warm water. Stroke each brush gently over a cake of soap several times in a back-and-forth motion to help loosen the paint. Stroke it several times across the palm of the hand to lather the brush, then rinse it in warm water. Shape the brush to a point with your fingers. Never use hot water; it tends to weaken brushes.

Although acrylics are water soluble, no amount of water can remove paint that has hardened on the bristles. In this instance, soak brushes for 20 minutes in a small amount of nailpolish remover (or in Aquatic or Craftint cleaners). Then wash them in mild soap and reshape the point with your fingers. Neglected brushes that have oil paints hardened on the bristles can be soaked in brush cleaner or paint remover, then washed and reshaped.

Acrylic paints

Acrylic paint is a water-soluble pigment mixed with a liquid plastic binder. It can be applied to any non-oily surface. With acrylics, the artist can achieve all the special effects that other mediums give. Opaque, warm and cool colors seem to come to life in acrylic paints. Transparent colors are used for glazing, which is described in chapter 13.

Acrylic paint has several advantages over other paints, including oils and water-based paints such as tempera, watercolors, casein, and egg-based paints. These paints have a tendency to flake and chip when heavily applied, but acrylic paint does not fade or peel from a rigid surface. Wood is used predominately in decorative painting, and often an antique is found where paint has flaked. When restoring these pieces, the problem of flaking is solved by using these nonflaking permanent plastic paints. Acrylics are also waterproof, and the colors cannot bleed into each other. A mistake can be corrected by painting directly over another color; the colors go on over each other without a muddy effect. Another advantage of using acrylics is that clean-up is so easy. Water and mild soap will clean your hands and brushes.

Acrylic paint dries in minutes, making it a fast medium to work with. Moisture evaporates rapidly on a dry day, but there is a slightly slower drying process on a humid day. If you wish the paint to remain moist longer, squeeze a generous amount on the palette. A protective film will form over the color mound, and the paint underneath will remain moist and workable. Leave the skin on top, and push your brush into the paint from the bottom of the mound. There are paint additives for lengthy projects if the color mound method is not preferred. A liquid retarder sprayed or dropped with eye dropper into the color will keep it moist.

Acrylic paint varies in consistency according to the manufacturer. Through trial and error, I found Grumbacher Hyplar Acrylics to be of the creamiest type and the best for this kind of painting. They excel over other name brands for coverage. If you should want to experiment with others, I would advise you to become familiar with all brands. Though acrylics come in many colors, the eleven below are all that are required for painting. Learn to mix all hues using only these few—it is a fine lesson in color mixing.

Titanium White	Permanent Green Light
Hansa Yellow Medium	Manganese Blue
Yellow Ochre	Ultramarine Blue
Hansa Orange	Burnt Sienna
Grumbacher Red	Mars Black
Thalo Crimson	

Replace caps after every use. For caps that are difficult to remove, light a match and hold it under the cap a few seconds to loosen it.

Oil paints

Artist's tube oil paints, which are used in tole painting, can be purchased at all art supply stores. I have listed all the colors you will need for painting. There are many more colors available, but buying them would inhibit your learning to mix colors yourself. Endless hues may be mixed with only these eleven colors. Purchase the white paint in the largest size as it is the most frequently used.

Titanium White	Permanent Green Light
Cadmium Yellow Medium	Cerulean Blue
Yellow Ochre	Ultramarine Blue
Cadmium Orange	Burnt Sienna
Grumbacher Red	Ivory Black
Alizarin Crimson	

Select only quality oils for lasting effectiveness. Inexpensive paints tend to crack and peel, and they may be too oily. Squeeze tube colors from the bottom to prevent air pockets from forming. Replace caps immediately after using. If a cap should become difficult to remove, hold a lighted match under it for a few seconds, then loosen.

Working with color

Color mixing is the fun part of painting, and becomes easy only when you know what you are seeing. The wide range of colors often leave the student feeling timid about painting. Color needs understanding to be used properly. I relate the use of color to the piano keys. Strike a key on the piano and a lovely tone is heard. Strike a wrong key next, and the first tone loses its beauty. Colors must be in tune with each other for the components to work together. One color should complement the other.

Invest in a color chart—it will help you to understand how the many color combinations work. There are three primary colors: red, blue and yellow. When these three primaries are mixed together equally, the result is a neutral grey. White added to this combination will result in lighter tones of grey. Colors can be mixed to achieve a variety of hues. Hue means color, and value means the degree of darkness or lightness. A complementary color on the circular color chart is the color directly opposite the primary color. For example, primary yellow is complementary to violet, and red is the complement of green. When red and green are mixed with each other, the primary red is slightly greyed by the cooler green color. This effect will be found in mixing any two complementary colors.

The use of warm and cool colors will teach you how color combinations work together. It is the foundation of all painting. Warm colors are sun colors. The sun produces red, yellow and orange. Orange is made by mixing red and yellow together, making it a secondary color. (All colors made from the primaries are called secondary colors.) The cool colors are from nature—blue and green. Primary blue added to primary yellow makes a secondary color of green. Blue can be warmed by adding a tint of red, giving it a slightly purple cast. Cool colors have warm complements.

Using colors in a monochromatic family is the use of one color and its many tones. The tones are created by adding very small amounts of warm and cool colors to the original color. For example, red, a dominant color, is cooled by adding green. White is then added for a variety of softer tones. Yellow ochre added to red with white produces a pleasing combination when used with the original red. Experiment on paper with warm and cool combinations, using one dominant color. Start with the primary colors, and try to use colors that are in harmony with each other.

Color theory takes practice, but it is basically simple because colors react to each other in predictable ways. Once the theory is understood, you will become aware of surrounding warms and cools. Study all the color illustrations in this book, and become aware of how many warm and cool hues have been used together. And study nature—after all, it is the source of all our colors and color combinations.

LAYING OUT THE PALETTE

Laying out the palette colors in a standard order is most efficient for the beginner. Like typing, one eventually knows where each color

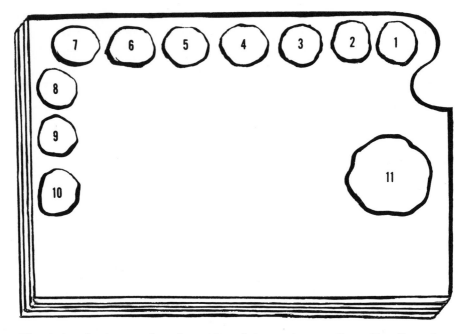

Fig. 4–1. *Laying out the palette. (1) cadmium or hansa yellow; (2) yellow ochre; (3) cadmium or hansa orange; (4) Grumbacher red; (5) alizarin or thalo crimson; (6) permanent green light; (7) cerulean or manganese blue; (8) ultramarine blue; (9) burnt sienna; (10) black; (11) white.*

sits on the palette, and the hand reaches for a specific color automatically. Start to lay the colors from right to left at the top of the palette (figure 4-1). Squeeze an amount about the size of a dime. Always squeeze the lightest color first, cadmium or hansa yellow medium in the upper right corner. Continue with yellow ochre, cadmium or hansa orange, Grumbacher red, alizarin or thalo crimson, permanent green light, cerulean or manganese blue, ultramarine blue, burnt sienna, and black. White is the most frequently used color, so squeeze an amount the size of a fifty-cent piece to the far right along the center. White should sit alone so there is less chance of its running into other colors. Mix all colors in the clean area in the center of the palette. When working with oils, it is important to use a palette knife for mixing to save wear and tear on your brushes. Acrylics can be mixed with your brush.

MIXING COLORS

Here are a few color combinations to help you with your painting. Specific recipes for colors commonly seen in folk painting are given later in the chapter.

Yellow and yellow ochre

White added to yellow and orange will give a peach tone.

Orange added to yellow ochre with a small amount of green will give you a mustardy gold.

White is added to yellow for lemon yellow.

White is added to yellow ochre for beige.

Red

Red is a favorite color in folk art. It can also be used as a good greying color when added to blues and greens.

Add white and yellow ochre to red for flesh tones.

Add white to red for tints of pink.

Blue is added to red to darken.

Yellow is added to red to lighten or make orange.

Add white to crimson for a bright pink.

Add a little white to blue and crimson for violet.

Black is added to red for rich rust tones.

Green

Permanent green light is your best green because it is neutral and can be shaded either lighter or darker than other greens.

Add yellow ochre and a little red to green for olive green. White will lighten hue.

Burnt sienna is added to green for dark, rich green for leaves, trees, lawns and shading.

Yellow ochre is added to above mixture for highlights on trees and foliage.

Blue is added to green for a turquoise; add white for aqua.

[27]

Burnt sienna

Use as a rich rust color alone.

Yellow ochre is added to burnt sienna for a lighter beige rust.

Black is added to burnt sienna for burnt umber.

Green is added to burnt sienna for dark green.

Blue

Ultramarine blue is used as a darkener and for intense hues.

Red is added to blue for purple.

White is added to purple for violet.

Black is added to blue for a dark blue.

White is added for a variety of blue shades.

Green and a little white is added for Prussian blue.

Green is added with a little red and white for a cool grey.

Black

Use black as an accent and for greying. Do not outline art in black, as it will create a hard line.

Yellow is added to black for olive green.

White is added to black for cold grey.

Yellow is added to cool grey for warm grey.

Red, blue and white with a tint of black creates a violet grey.

COLOR FORMULAS

Color formulas make it easy for the beginner to achieve bright and pleasing colors as opposed to muddy tones which occur when the wrong combinations of colors are used. The combinations listed below are used for flesh tones, hair, flowers, fruit, clothing, and backgrounds.

Flesh: 8 parts white, 1 part red, 1 part yellow ochre.

Lips and cheeks: 6 parts white, 2 parts red, 2 parts yellow ochre.

Light blonde hair: 8 parts yellow ochre, 2 parts white.

Dark blonde hair: 5 parts yellow ochre, 5 parts burnt sienna.

Light redhead: 8 parts orange, 2 parts white.

Dark redhead: 7 parts Grumbacher red, 3 parts orange.

Light brown hair: 5 parts burnt sienna, 5 parts yellow ochre.

Dark brown hair: 5 parts burnt sienna, 2 parts ultramarine blue.

Dark green: 7 parts permanent green light, 3 parts burnt sienna.

Light green: 5 parts permanent green light, 4 parts yellow ochre, 1 part white.

Olive green: 8 parts Hansa or cadmium yellow medium, 2 parts black.

Light pink rose: 6 parts thalo or alizarin crimson, 4 parts white.

Dark rose: 9 parts thalo or alizarin crimson, 1 part white.

Warm light blue: 7 parts ultramarine blue, 3 parts white.

Cool light blue: 7 parts manganese or cerulean blue, 3 parts white.

Turquoise: 4 parts manganese or cerulean blue, 4 parts permanent green light, 2 parts white.

Dark blue: 8 parts ultramarine blue, 2 parts burnt sienna.

Prussian blue: 6 parts ultramarine blue, 3 parts permanent green light, 1 part white.

Lavender: 4 parts ultramarine blue, 4 parts thalo or alizarin crimson, 2 parts white.

Rust: 8 parts Grumbacher red, 2 parts black.

Antique red: 7 parts thalo or alizarin crimson, 3 parts yellow ochre.

Deep red: 7 parts thalo or alizarin crimson, 3 parts burnt sienna.

Cool grey: 5 parts manganese blue, 2 parts Grumbacher red, 2 parts yellow ochre, 1 part white.

Warm grey: 5 parts ultramarine blue, 2 parts Grumbacher red, 2 parts yellow ochre, 1 part white.

Grey green: 5 parts permanent green light, 2 parts ultramarine blue, 2 parts yellow ochre, 1 part white.

5

The Acrylic and Mud Painting Method

Acrylic and mud is a completely new method of decorative painting. The richness and depth of the old world school of painting is achieved with a minimum of color blending and the use of a "mud" stain. This new method can be applied to any design.

The acrylic and mud method of painting uses a stain with the consistency of thick mud over the painted work. This gives the art work the dimension and richness, unobtainable with paint alone, needed to achieve the antique look of the old world. The mud stain is not used in tole painting, as shading is done by blending colors.

Decorative painting techniques

The stain is applied after the art work has dried, so let's do the painting first. Here's a rundown of the materials you will need to decorate a piece with the acrylic and mud technique:

Prepared wood or metal surface for painting, or paper for practice.
Brushes and paints recommended in chapter 4.
Acrylic paper palette—a shiny surface for mixing colors.
Mud stain—used for shading finished art.

Linseed oil—used to remove mud.

Low-lustre varnish or polyurethane—used for final finish coat.

0000 steel wool—used between coats of varnish for a hand-rubbed effect.

Water cup

Turpentine

Paper towels

Varnish brush—a 2-inch bristle brush. Use only for varnishing. Can be purchased in any paint store. Clean this brush in turpentine, then wash in soap and warm water.

Mud brush—a 1- or 2-inch bristle brush. Use only for mudding. Do not wash or clean; wrap in airtight tin foil, and store in freezer until needed. The brush can also be stored in a small amount of turpentine, but the fumes could be objectionable.

Before you begin to paint, place your colors, brushes, palette, and palette knife in front of you. Lay out the palette as described in chapter 4. Be sure you are sitting at a comfortable table—a tilt-top drawing table is best. You will find you can work longer hours if you sit upright rather than hunched over a flat table.

White paper toweling should always be kept handy to wipe brushes. Test your brush after using each color by washing it thoroughly and wiping it on the white toweling. If the towel appears slightly discolored, the brush must be washed again until no trace of color comes off on towel. Right-handed artists should place the palette to the right of the table, and left-handed artists should place it on the left. Keep a water cup near the palette.

When mixing paint, be sure the consistency is creamy. Test the paint on paper to be sure it is opaque. If it is too thick and forms ridges, use a few drops of water to thin it. If the paint is too thin and transparent, add more paint.

As we'll learn later in this chapter, the mud or antique mixture is used on the art work for shading. Often, however, artists like to blend colors with acrylics to enhance the shading. Acrylics blend well, and can be worked into each other when wet, or applied over dry colors. Work toward using bold colors and bright highlights with the acrylic and mud technique, because the mud stain tends to tone down the colors.

If you are a beginner, choose a simple design to paint. Get a feel for design outlines and shapes by sketching still lifes of fruit or flowers. Also practice painting individual fruits on paper. This will help you to see and analyze colors as well as shapes. Refer often to your color chart, and study color combinations to familiarize yourself with proper values. Improper combinations will result in muddy colors and aggravation. Practice color combinations on paper by painting flowers and fruits.

Use the #5 brush for all backgrounds, painting with back and forth strokes. Avoid many small strokes—brush marks may appear. Details should be painted over the background with the #2 brush. Painting the basic squiggle stroke and various fruits and flowers is described below. Once you can do them successfully, you are ready for anything.

THE SQUIGGLE

The squiggle is the shape of a thousand designs (figures 5-1—5-3). It dates back to the original folk art period, and is sometimes referred to as the key or basic stroke. Its shape resembles a tear drop, and it is often used to fill blank areas. Several squiggles combined will create flowers, hearts, borders, leaves—almost all the basic designs seen in folk painting.

There are several different approaches to making the basic stroke. Some use a flat bristle brush, others a camel hair brush, but I find a red sable pointed watercolor brush is the easiest for the beginner. It takes practice, but it is mastered easily.

To begin, squeeze a small amount of acrylic paint on the palette. Add very little water, just enough to create a creamy consistency. Use a #5 brush to learn the basic stroke. After some practice, you may want to use a #2 brush for delicate squiggles. Dip the brush into the paint, then roll it on the palette to take off any excess paint. Hold the brush straight up and steady your hand by resting on the small finger. Begin the stroke at the point of the squiggle, placing the point of brush on the paper. Pull the brush along slowly, placing more pressure on the brush as you go (figure 5-6). Controlling the pressure of brush is the

Fig. 5–1. *Squiggles: a basic folk painting stroke.*

Fig. 5–2. *More squiggle shapes.*

Fig. 5–3.   *Combining squiggles will create endless patterns and shapes.*

Fig. 5—4.   *The paisley pattern is a combination of squiggles.*

[36]

Fig. 5–5. *Squiggles can become flowers and birds.*

Fig. 5–6. *Controlling the brush pressure is the key to the squiggle.*

key to the squiggle. Increasing the pressure broadens the stroke. Practice many squiggles before you work on wood, and try your hand at curved ones.

Once you've mastered this stroke, work it into patterns. Try simple ones first, such as tulips, leaves and borders. Figure 5-5 shows how squiggles can become flowers and birds. Try more complicated designs as you progress, like the paisley pattern (figure 5-4). The paisley is an intricate combination of different squiggles, and is often used in conjunction with other designs. Experiment, and you will always discover new ideas.

HOW TO PAINT A ROSE

The cherished rose is used in folk art as frequently as the tulip. A rose can be painted in several different styles: symbolic, realistic, free-

Fig. 5–7. *How to paint a rose.*

hand, or the simple stroke method. However it is painted, it is a favorite design of all folk artists, and beginners should use it often.

A rose may be compared to a cup and saucer. The base petals are the saucer, and the center bud is the cup. Using a #2 brush, start with a middle value of pink, white, and Grumbacher red, and paint the entire rose shape as shown in figure 5-7. Then use thalo crimson, a dark red, to paint the center and the folds between the petals. Paint the center first, and work out toward the edges (figure 5-7). Mix white and a very small amount of Grumbacher red to paint highlights on the tips of the petals. The rose is completed by shading lightly around its right side and on the background close to flower. Shading is done with the mud stain, which is described later in this chapter. Two other styles of roses can be seen in the color section.

HOW TO PAINT A PEAR

The lovely pear, whether by itself or in groupings, lends itself beautifully to folk art. Pears are frequently used on chair backs, dining table borders, mirrors, chests, boxes, and in baskets. Design your own patterns using the pear. After you learn how to paint other fruits, combine them to make your own still life.

Begin the pear by painting the solid shape shown in figure 5-8 with yellow ochre. For a touch of added color on the right side, mix Grumbacher red with a small amount of yellow ochre. Use up and down strokes with a #5 brush to blend this tint, and work toward the

Fig. 5-8. *How to paint a pear.*

middle of the fruit. Mix a middle highlight of white with a small amount of hansa yellow, and paint it on the upper and lower left of the pear (see figure 5-8). For a bright highlight, blend a touch of white into the center of these middle highlights.

For the leaf, mix permanent green light with a bit of burnt sienna and lighten with white. Paint the leaf with a #5 brush using a squiggle stroke. Use burnt sienna and a #2 brush to paint the stem and leaf veins. Finish the pear by shading its right side with the mud technique and blend the stain toward the middle of the fruit.

HOW TO PAINT GRAPES

Grapes are the unifying shape for most fruit designs. The grouping of grapes holds a pattern together and keeps the rest of the fruit from "floating," or appearing disjointed. Often designs appear weak,

Fig. 5-9. *How to paint grapes. Blend the mud stain with your finger.*

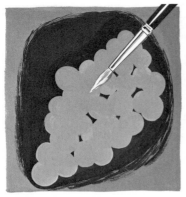
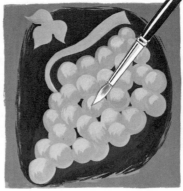
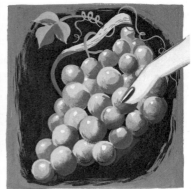

and look as though they could fall off the paper. Grapes give a design a base to work from; they are the most useful of fruits in a grouping.

The acrylic and mud method becomes a fun game using the thumb to place the grapes on a background. Paint a black background in the shape of a cluster of grapes. This will give the finished painting a stronger depth when it is mudded. Mix a green grape color of white, yellow ochre, and a small amount of permanent green light. Stick your thumb in the paint pool, then make a thumbprint over the black background to form a grape. Start at the top to create the cluster of grapes, and continue to the bottom ending with one grape (see figure 5-9). Acrylics dry quickly, so keep your thumb coated with fresh paint.

Using a #2 brush, fill in the grapes with the green grape color. Mix white with the green grape color to make a middle highlight and paint it on the left side of each grape, as shown in figure 5-9. For bright highlights, add a white dot to the middle highlights.

Paint the stem using a #2 brush and a mixture of yellow ochre and burnt sienna. Mix yellow ochre and permanent green light for the leaf and paint it using the squiggle technique and a #5 brush. Paint the tendrils light green with a #2 brush.

Add a strong contrast between the dark right side and the highlighted left side of each grape with the mud stain.

HOW TO PAINT AN APPLE

The apple is one of the simplest fruits to paint with the acrylic and mud method, and works well in many decorative designs.

Fig. 5–10. *How to paint an apple.*

Paint the entire apple shape shown in figure 5-10 with Grumbacher red. Highlight the left side with a mixture of white and orange, and brighten the center of the highlight with white (see figure 5-10). Paint the leaf an olive green color by mixing yellow ochre, green and a touch of red. Add white to this mixture for light green veins. The stem is a mixture of burnt sienna and blue. Shade the right side darkly with the mud stain for depth.

HOW TO PAINT STRAWBERRIES

Strawberries are a delight to paint. The vivid red and green are enough to enhance any design.

The basic shape to begin painting your strawberries with is a modified version of a Valentine heart with a rounded point (figure 5-11). Using a #2 pointed brush, paint the entire strawberry with Grumbacher red. For middle highlights, mix white with small amounts of red and orange, and paint the left sides of the strawberries. For the brightest highlights, use pure white paint in the center of the middle highlights. Using a #2 brush, paint black dots to indicate seeds on the berries everywhere except in the highlights. On the left side of each black dot, paint a white dot for a highlight. Mix green and yellow ochre with white for the leaves, and mix burnt sienna and blue for the stems. Shade the right side of the strawberry with the mud stain. Highlights should be free of mud.

Fig. 5–11.   How to paint strawberries. Mud stain can be blended with your finger.

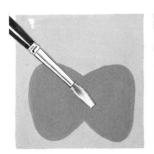 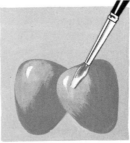  

Fig. 5–12. *How to paint a tulip. Blend the mud stain with your finger.*

HOW TO PAINT A TULIP

Tulips have been used more frequently in folk art than any other flower as borders, added decoration, or as the main theme for a pattern. The acrylic and mud method is very effective for this flower.

To create a simple tulip, make two fat squiggles joined in the center (see figure 5-12). Use a #5 pointed brush and a mixture of manganese blue, permanent green light, and white for a turquoise color. Paint the top stamen thalo crimson, and the bud at bottom of the flower black. Mix an olive green from yellow medium and black for the leaves and stem.

Highlight the left side of the flower with white mixed with a small amount of turquoise. Highlight the leaves with white mixed with a small amount of olive green. Shade the right side of the tulip with mud and blend it with your finger for softness.

Distressing

Distressing is another term for gouging the wood for a worn, aged appearance. Distress your piece after the painted design has dried thoroughly and before applying the mud stain. The mud antiquing works with the distress marks to create a lovely patina of age.

[43]

Fig. 5–13. *Gouge the wood lightly in the same direction as its grain.*

Any number of tools can be used for distressing—a file, awl, nail, screwdriver, or sharp scissor. Study the wood grain direction. Although the piece has been base coated and decorated, it should be easy to see the direction that the wood grain runs in. With a sharp instrument, dig gently into the wood in the same direction of the grain (see figure 5-13). A gouge of half an inch is all that is necessary. Make several gouges; five or six will do. Never gouge over the design, however—work on the background only.

The mud stain

The mud stain method described here can be used on metal as well as wood. Applied over the decorative painting and distressing, the mud creates subtle shading effects and gives the entire piece an antiqued appearance. The second color figure illustrates the dramatic improvement mud staining can make. Remember to use predominantly bold colors with plenty of highlights, since the mud stain tends to tone down the colors. Though the process is a bit messy, the results will be well worth your efforts.

Do not use commercial stains from kits purchased in paint stores. Their colors do not provide the proper shading, and their consistency is too thin to be workable. It took me a year of trial and error to come up with the correct color and consistency for this mud stain.

To make the mud stain, simply mix one quart of burnt umber oil-based pigment with one quart of oil-based liquid clear glaze. Both can be bought in paint stores. Stir thoroughly with a mixing stick and pour the stain into 4-ounce baby food jars. Storing the stain in small jars makes it easier to handle. Rub the inside rim of the lids with petroleum jelly before capping to make removing them easier. You can store the stain for several years. A little goes a long way, so use it sparingly.

The art work should be completely dry before you stain it. Spread the mud stain over the entire art work and background with a 2-inch brush. Then wipe the whole surface with a clean cloth or paper towel. It's a good idea to wear rubber gloves while doing this. Leave a film of stain over the entire surface, with a bit more around the edges.

Begin shading the art work immediately, before the mud stain has dried. Use small amounts of linseed oil on a clean cloth, and rub in a circular motion to remove mud to the desired shade. Leave more mud in and around grooves to accent them (figure 5-14). Shade the background so that it darkens toward the edges and is darker to the right of the art work (figure 5-15). Fruits and flowers should be shaded on the right side and lighter toward the middle. Do not allow shading on the left side or in the highlighted areas; the right side should contrast greatly with the left. The light areas will add lustre, while the shaded areas will give depth to the art work (figure 5-16). For delicate shading in small areas, use a facial tissue, a cotton swab, or your finger. Blending the shades with the soft padding of your finger produces a soft finish.

View your art work through a mirror to see if the shading has created the desired effects. This little trick allows you to see your work

Fig. 5–14. *The mud stain accents grooves and edges.*

Fig. 5–15. *The background should become darker toward the edges.*

Fig. 5–16. *The shading on this flower creates depth.*

with added dimension. Errors in shading will show up more easily. If you need darker shading, apply a bit more mud with a brush or cloth. If areas need to be lightened, rub them with linseed oil. Blend for a final smoothness with your finger.

This stain has many uses other than decorative painting. It may be used on furniture to cover scratches. Simply rub over the scratches with a small amount on a cloth. For darkening floors and steps, dilute the stain slightly with linseed oil. Rub the stain on with a cloth, and wipe it off with a clean cloth. You can even use the stain as burnt umber when painting on canvas.

Varnishing

When the stained object is thoroughly dry (wait at least 24 hours), it is ready for the final step of varnishing. Varnish only on a dry day; humidity will interfere with drying. Gently stir the varnish with a stick in a figure-eight motion. Fast stirring causes bubbles. Dip the brush into the center of the can (if the brush touches the rim of the can, bubbles may form on the brush). Place the varnish-filled brush in the center of the object and stroke or flow the varnish in one direction toward the outer edges. Do not use a back and forth motion, or bubbles may form.

Carefully lift the object from underneath and raise it above your head to check for drippings of varnish. Smooth any drips with the brush. Set varnished object a few inches off the table, resting on two cans or a piece of wood. Allow 24 hours drying time. When thoroughly dry, use 0000 steel wool, and rub gently over the entire area to remove any particles. Use a tack cloth to remove loose particles of steel wool.

Repeat this procedure several times. A wall plaque or other decorative item is best with three coats of varnish; furniture is best with five. Buff the finished piece with a soft, clean cloth.

To store varnish, tap several holes in the rim of the can with a nail. Excess varnish will drip into the can through the holes, and lid will fit airtight. Tap the lid with a hammer to insure a tight fit.

[47]

6

The Tole Painting Method

Tole painting originally referred to the early French technique of decorating tinware that was painted with a black chemical to retard rust. Today we use the term to mean the freehand style of decorative folk art painting that uses tube oil paints rather than acrylics. Brush stroke painting, folk art painting, decorative painting, and country painting are other names sometimes given to this method.

The liveliness and depth of tole painting depend on the blending and shading of colors. Color blending may begin right from the start by loading the brush with more than one shade, or else a single color may be brushed on and then others added and blended with it. This is easy to do with oils because they dry so slowly. No mud or antique stain is used to alter the character of the tole painting. The piece is varnished in the same way as described in chapter 5 for acrylic-painted pieces.

Some of the earliest furniture in America decorated by tole painting was discovered in New England, Connecticut, and Pennsylvania (figure 6-1). The Connecticut River Valley produced fascinating chests, boxes and tinware reminiscent of the Flemish and French decorations. The French developed designs of elaborate scrollwork, sophisticated birds, exquisite flower groupings, and patterns of crewel-type designs. The scrollwork used on our American dollar was originated by the French.

The Pennsylvania Germans, rich with a heritage of old-world peas-

Fig. 6–1. *Typical American tole designs.*

ant designs, gave us some of our most treasured patterns (figure 6-2). Their motifs, mainly symbolic, brought us the unicorns, guardians of maidenhood. The "tree of life" design expresses the continuation of birth, death, and reincarnation. Hex signs, so prevalent on barns in Pennsylvania, were painted in vibrant hues to ward off evil spirits. Hearts were used as the symbol of love using the color red, sacred to Donar, god of marriage and home. The Pennsylvania Dutch also gave us the everloving tulip as a symbol of the Trinity. The cherished rose was a favorite of the Scandinavians, and was painted with a realistic appearance on chests, boxes, chairs, and tinware. The practice became known as rosemahling; mahling is the Scandinavian word for painting.

The technique of tole consists of several varieties of brush strokes to create leaves, flowers, birds, figures, and fruit. The strokes are simple, and are similar to the squiggle discussed in chapter 5. Often one stroke creates the design, such as a leaf. It is an exhilarating style of painting for both beginner and advanced student. The freehand technique has charm and grace, but also requires patience and practice.

Getting started

Gather all supplies together. Have the following materials at hand before you begin painting:

Prepared wood or metal surface for painting, or paper for practice.

Brushes and oil paints recommended in chapter 4.

Palette—purchase a paper palette for easy clean-up. Tear off sheet and throw away after use.

Palette knife—used for mixing paint on palette to save wear on brushes.

Cobalt dryer—add two to six drops of dryer to oil paint to hasten drying time. This is especially important in high altitudes or humid areas. Use sparingly.

Copal painting medium—used to thin colors slightly. Keeps paint at even consistency for a longer period of time when working on a lengthy project. Apply with eye dropper.

Fig. 6–2. *Pennsylvania Dutch tole paintings.*

Gum spirits of turpentine—used for thinning and cleaning brushes.

Small cup—for the copal medium.

Paper towels—for wiping brushes as you paint.

Low-lustre varnish or polyurethane, 0000 steel wool, and a 2-inch varnish brush.

Be sure to wear a smock for cover-up and sit at a comfortable table. This is very important—a tired artist will never produce quality work. If you are right-handed, you'll want to have the palette to the right of your work table. If you are left-handed, keep the palette to your left.

Loading the brush

Since no mud or antique stain is used in tole painting, all shading, color blending and finishing must be done with the oil paints. Colors are blended either on the palette or on the painted surface. Color highlights and mixtures of warm and cool colors provide shading for your tole designs. You can also create unique shading effects by varying the texture of your brush strokes and the thickness with which you apply the paint. You'll want to practice and experiment often on paper to master the many possibilities of oil paints.

For each painting session, lay out the palette in the order described in chapter 4. Mix all colors in the clean area in the center of the palette using the palette knife. Mix colors with copal medium to a consistency of whipped cream. Dip the knife into the mixture and lift—if small peaks form, you are ready to paint. Dip your brush in turpentine to soften it. For beginners, the paint should be slightly thinner than usual to practice the basic strokes. Add a few extra drops of medium to the color. This is also an excellent consistency for scrollwork, borders, ribbons and stems.

Use a #2 pointed brush to practice loading the brush with paint. Hold the brush low on its metal ferrule next to the hairs with your thumb, index and middle fingers. Let your arm swing freely from the

Contemporary folk art design, using the acrylic and mud technique.

Mud staining procedure. Brush "mud" stain on the decorated surface, then rub away the mud with linseed oil and towel, letting some stain remain to shade the edges and the central design.

Basic strokes for tole painting, showing blending of colors.

Two ways to paint a rose. Top: using a controlled stroke. Bottom: freehand style.

Fruits painted in the tole style, using blending of colors to create shading and highlighting.

Squiggles of all sizes are a major element in this Spanish-inspired angel. Painted on a wood or metal object, the design can be further enhanced with a mud stain.

This stylized arrangement has a stenciled effect. Much of the coloring is achieved not by blending colors on the palette but by placing different colors next to each other in the design elements.

Beginner's portrait painting.

Advanced portrait painting.

An arrangement of fruit. Acrylic and mud on wood.

Wooden box decorated with dancing figures. Acrylic and mud technique.

Antique shoe. Actually a mass-produced plaster replica, primed with gesso and decorated in acrylic and mud method.

Wooden chairs were traditionally enlivened with simple motifs. Here a more elaborate scene decorates a chair seat.

Decorator's mirror, with rosebud nosegay. Acrylic and mud on wood.

Decorative panel. Acrylic and mud on wood.

An old hutch, stripped and decorated to make a unique piece of furniture.

Tree ornament hang-me-ups.

Two counter-top scales.
Acrylic and mud on metal.

Hand mirror. Acrylic and
mud on wood.

"Welcome to our house"
tray. Acrylic and mud on
wood.

shoulder with your elbow raised up and out. Using a swinging pendulum motion, drag one side of the brush along the outside edge of the paint pool. Stroke the brush several times in one direction, pressing it deeper into the pool of paint. Short strokes are sufficient. Load flat brushes in the same manner.

To blend colors as they paint, artists often load the brush with two colors at once. Load each side of the brush with a different color, being careful not to smear them together. As you practice your strokes, turn the brush slowly, taking note of how the colors blend. Practice blending many different colors until you can predict and control the results.

Basic strokes

Six basic strokes are needed to create most shapes in tole painting: the squiggle, S-shape, crescent, double-pointed, knife, and broad (see the third color figure). The strokes are controlled by varying the pressure on the brush. The position of the hand on the brush is most important. Keep your hand low on the metal ferrule next to the bristles.

Load a #2 pointed brush with two colors to practice the squiggle stroke (top left in the color figure; see also figures 5-2 and 5-4). Start at the point of the squiggle, using very little pressure, and draw the brush away from you, using more pressure on the wide part of the squiggle. Most methods have students start at the wide part and work towards them. I've found that students using my technique have an easier time painting, and that the squiggles are crisper and cleaner. Practice making straight squiggles, too, like the one in the lower right corner of the third color figure.

The S stroke is often used for borders and in combinations of flowers and petals. To make the S stroke, use a flat #4 brush. Hold the brush low on the metal ferrule and in a perpendicular position. Turn it to the narrow, knife side for a fine line and start at the top of the S. Draw the brush down using more pressure towards the center. As you come to the center and continue to the bottom, twist the brush gently to the broad side, then twist back to the knife edge and lift slowly. Practice this stroke often; it is as useful as the ever-popular squiggle.

[53]

To make the crescent in one stroke, start at a point, bear down to make the wide part of the shape, and then ease up on the pressure again to end at a point. The crescent shape may be made in two or three strokes if that is easier for you, or you can try outlining and filling in. It is best, however, to control the shape of your strokes by controlling the pressure on the brush.

The double-pointed stroke is also made with a light–heavy–light pressure on the brush, similar to the execution of the crescent, except it is straight instead of curved.

Use your smallest brush to make the narrow, knife-like stripe. This stroke requires a very light pressure from beginning to end. Simply lift your brush at the end to finish the stroke.

To make the broad, straight, round-ended stroke in the color figure, lay the brush down with full pressure. This should give you a rounded shape at the beginning of the stroke. Then drag straight down with even pressure, and at the end, twist the brush very slightly to round the base.

Practice blending the colors on the brush as you make your strokes, so you get effects like those in the color figure. Aim for a textured stroke of light and dark shades. Pressure is the key to making these strokes. Do not be afraid to apply enough pressure to fill out the brush properly, and to use force when needed in painting. Do not be timid—mistakes are meant to be learned from. When you've mastered these strokes, try them in combination with each other, as in the stylized flower shown in the color figure.

Painting fruit

Once you feel you have mastered the basic strokes, practice painting the fruits shown in the fifth color figure. Color blending the fruits creates shading and highlights that seem to bring the fruit to life.

First paint the shape of each fruit a basic overall color. For example, the apple can be Grumbacher red. On the darker right side use alizarin red blended halfway toward the middle of the fruit. The highlight on the left side consists of white and Grumbacher red mixed together. Finish with a short dab of white for the brightest highlight.

Mistakes can be easily remedied by a method called wiping out. Fill a #2 pointed brush with turpentine, stroke over the paint to be removed, and wipe away with a soft tissue.

Practice painting the leaf designs shown in color several times in a variety of color blendings. Load the brush with a basic color, such as permanent light green mixed with yellow ochre, and paint the entire leaf. Wash the brush, then highlight the tip of the leaf with a mixture of white and light green.

Also practice painting leaves with two colors loaded onto your brush. For the darker color, mix a little Grumbacher red into permanent green light. Mix yellow ochre and permanent green light for the lighter shade. Fill opposite sides of the brush with the two colors. To paint a squiggle leaf, start at its lower point and keep the side of the brush with the darker shade to the right. Draw the brush across the leaf with increasing pressure, and twist the brush slightly to blend the colors.

Painting flowers

Painting a flower in the tole method is very similar to painting flowers in the acrylic method (chapter 5). Begin by painting the basic shape of the flower with the predominant color. Using highlights and shading hues, gradually fill in the petals and all the details. Figure 6-3 shows how to paint a field flower and a rose. Carefully imitate the sequence shown in the figure to achieve similar results.

The fourth color figure shows two kinds of roses, the most popular flower in tole. Pinks are usually used for roses because they are warm colors and work well with other floral hues. The top rose in the figure is based on the squiggle stroke, each squiggle representing a petal around the center of the flower. (Note how the flower center is painted at the *top* of the blossom in this view.) The other rose blossom in the color figure is painted in a freehand style, like that in figure 6-3. Try to imitate the strokes and shadings of color in these blossoms. Once you've mas-

[55]

Fig. 6–3. *Painting a field flower and a rose.*

tered them, you will be ready to experiment with painting other kinds of flowers.

Painting flowers by the tole method is a great way to express your creativity. Figure 6-4 offers several different styles and shapes for you to

Fig. 6-4.   *A variety of flower shapes.*

Fig. 6–5. *Several styles of flowers compose an interesting bouquet.*

Fig. 6–6. *The tulip is the center of attraction in the stylized floral design.*

Fig. 6–7. *Fruits, flowers, and leaves combined in borders.*

practice with. Experiment with different color blends and strokes, and come up with your own designs. Don't keep using the same kind of rose or tulip in all your designs. (Nothing is more tiresome than using the same type of flower over and over again.)

Figures 6-5, 6-6, and 6-7 show how different styles of flowers, leaves, and fruits can be combined in designs and borders. Daisies are the simplest flowers to paint. The petals are nothing more than an arrangement of squiggle strokes around a center. Daisies are often used in groupings with other flowers as fill-ins (see figure 6-5). Used alone they make interesting borders.

Tulips are borrowed from our early American artists, and are almost as popular as the rose. Use them often, as the grace of these beautifully designed flowers charms any piece they adorn (see figure 6-6).

7

Vegetables and Herbs

Vegetables can be painted in either the tole or acrylic method. For the extra practice, both techniques should be tried. Use #5 pointed brush and paint in broad, even strokes. Trace the illustrations in this chapter for patterns; colors are suggested for each vegetable. Refer to the color recipes in chapter 4 for a variety of combinations.

Once you have mastered the individual vegetables, paint them together as a still life (figure 7-1). This is the best experience for an artist. The more designs you practice compiling and grouping, the faster you will learn to see design and balance. Use paper for practice before painting on wood or metal.

Vegetables

TOMATOES

Paint the entire shape of the tomato with Grumbacher red. For the shadow, use thalo crimson. Highlight using a mixture of yellow ochre with a little orange. For leaves, use a touch of white and yellow ochre with permanent green light.

[62]

Fig. 7–1. *Vegetables can decorate a simple plaque, or they can be part of a larger design.*

BEETS

Paint the entire area of beet with a mixture of Grumbacher red and a small amount of ultramarine blue. Paint the shaded side with a mixture of thalo or alizarin crimson and ultramarine blue. Highlight with a mix of white with a little red. Leaves are a mixture of permanent green light and yellow ochre. Veins on the leaves should be the same color as the beet—red.

GARLIC

Paint entire area of garlic with a mixture of white and a small amount of yellow ochre. For the shaded side, add a small amount of ultramarine blue. Paint the detail lines with this darker mixture.

GREEN PEPPERS

Paint entire area of the peppers with a mixture of permanent green light, manganese or cerulean blue, and a small amount of yellow ochre. For the shaded side, use permanent green light and a small amount of burnt sienna. Highlight with a mixture of white and a small amount of manganese or cerulean blue. Paint stem with mixture for shadows.

ONIONS

Paint entire area of onion with a mixture of yellow ochre, orange, and a small amount of white. For the shadow side of the onion, add a small amount of ultramarine blue. Paint the detail lines with this darker mixture.

CARROTS

Paint entire area of carrots with a mixture of orange plus yellow. Shade the carrots with a mix of red and orange. The leaves are a mixture of green and yellow ochre. Paint the veins of leaves with a darker tone of green mixed with red.

Fig. 7–2. Tomatoes, beet, garlic.

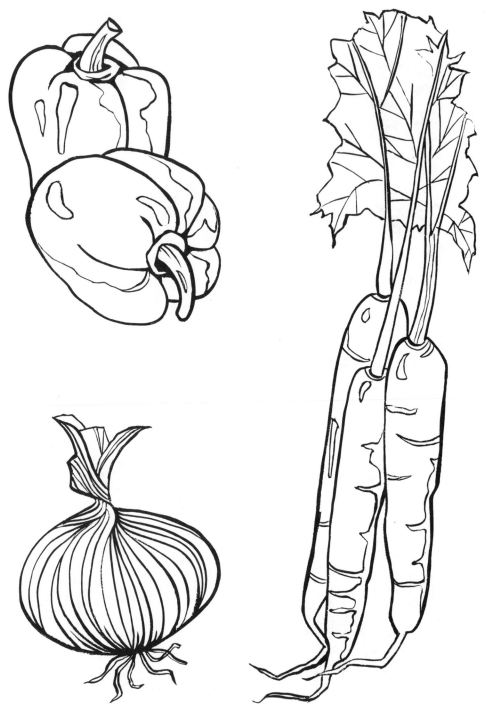

Fig. 7–3. *Green peppers, onion, carrots.*

[66]

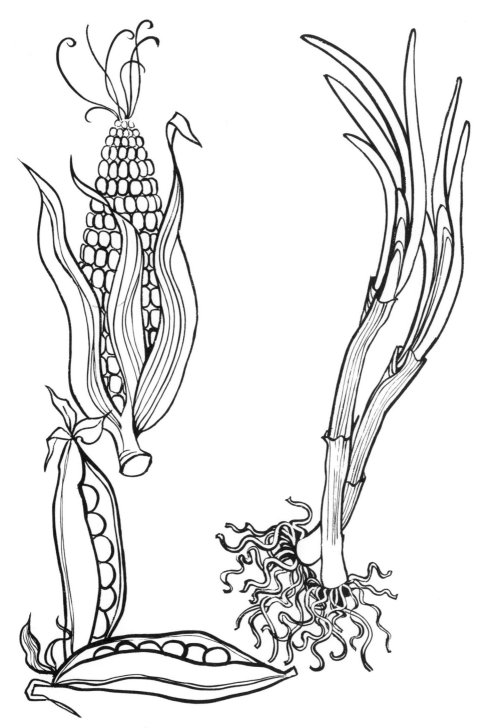

Fig. 7-4. *Corn, scallions, peas.*

CORN

Paint kernels with a clear yellow and small amount of white. Paint around each kernel with orange mixed with a small amount of green to darken. Paint husks with a mixture of green and yellow ochre with a touch of red. Use a small pointed brush to paint details of husks with green darkened with red. Use burnt sienna for corn silk.

SCALLIONS

Paint bottom of scallions with white and green mix, adding more white as you work toward the bottom. Upper leaves are a mix of green with a small amount of yellow ochre. Indicate detail lines with green and a touch of blue. Paint roots white.

PEAS

Paint inside of pod a darker shade of green using green with a touch of ultramarine blue. For the outside, mix green with a touch of yellow ochre. Peas are a mix of white, yellow and a touch of green.

GREEN BEANS

Paint beans with a mixture of green and a touch of yellow ochre. Paint shadows with a mixture of green and red, and a touch of manganese or cerulean blue. Add more yellow to the bean color for the stems.

RADISHES

Paint radishes with Grumbacher red. Shade right side with thalo or alizarin crimson added to red. Roots should be a lighter shade—mix white and a touch of red.

CUCUMBERS

Paint entire cucumber with a mixture of green and manganese or cerulean blue and a touch of yellow ochre. Shade with a small amount

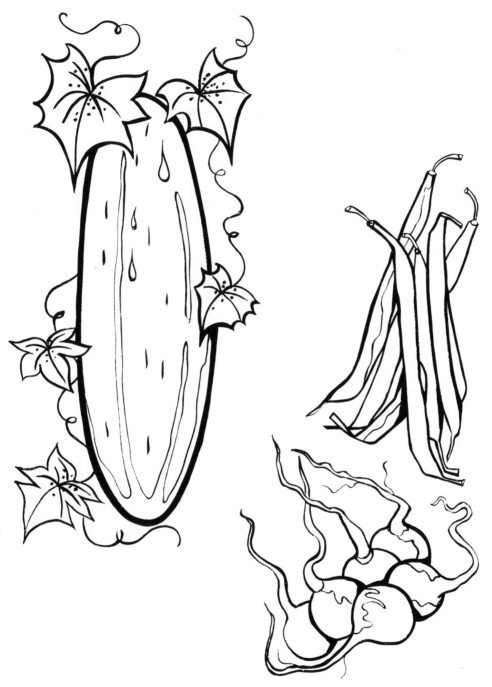

Fig. *7–5. Cucumber, green beans, radishes.*

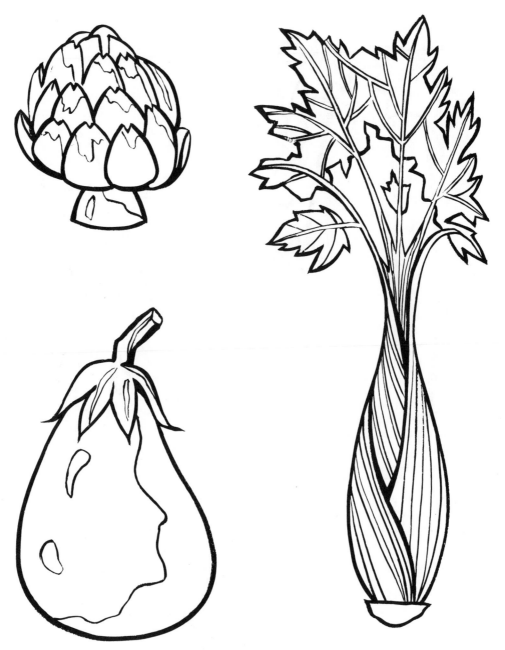

Fig. 7–6. *Artichoke, eggplant, celery.*

Fig. 7–7. *Acorn squash, summer squash, asparagus.*

of ultramarine blue added to the base color. Leaves are yellow ochre and green with a little white. Use more yellow for highlights.

EGGPLANT

Paint eggplant with a mixture of thalo or alizarin crimson and ultramarine blue. Shade with crimson and a touch of black. Highlight with white and a touch of manganese or cerulean blue. Stems and leaves are yellow ochre mixed with green and a touch of red.

ARTICHOKES

Paint artichoke with a mixture of green and a little yellow ochre. Shade under each petal with green and ultramarine blue. Highlight the tip of each petal with yellow ochre and green.

CELERY

Paint celery stalk with a mixture of green, yellow and white. Paint leaves with green and yellow ochre. Paint veins of leaves with basic color of celery. Using detail brush, paint detail lines with green and blue mix.

ACORN SQUASH

Paint entire squash with green, a touch of burnt sienna and a little yellow ochre. Shade with green, burnt sienna and ultramarine blue. Highlight with white, yellow ochre and a touch of green.

SUMMER SQUASH

Paint squash with yellow and a touch of white. Shade with yellow ochre and a touch of red. Use this mixture for the detail lines.

ASPARAGUS

Paint asparagus stalk with a mixture of green, yellow ochre and white. The scale-like leaves and head of the asparagus are painted a darker shade of green, yellow ochre and red.

Herbs

Herbs add a delicate, yet almost wild appearance to many designs (see figure 7-8). Their lovely leaves and blossoms have been used as decorative art on posters, in books, on greeting cards, and in many decorative borders. Learn to use the plants in your art work on furniture, mirrors, plaques, and odd pieces of wood. By themselves they often appear delicate and earthy. Added to flower arrangements and other designs, they flow through empty spaces with a lively effect.

Paint herbs with the same techniques you would use to paint fruits, flowers and leaves (see chapters 5 and 6). Remember, however, that you will be working on a much smaller scale. Use your smallest pointed brush, and a very delicate touch. For most herbs, you will want to maintain a free-flowing style and light texture with your brush work.

Fig. 7–8. *Herbs add a delicate, yet almost wild appearance to many designs.*

〔 74 〕

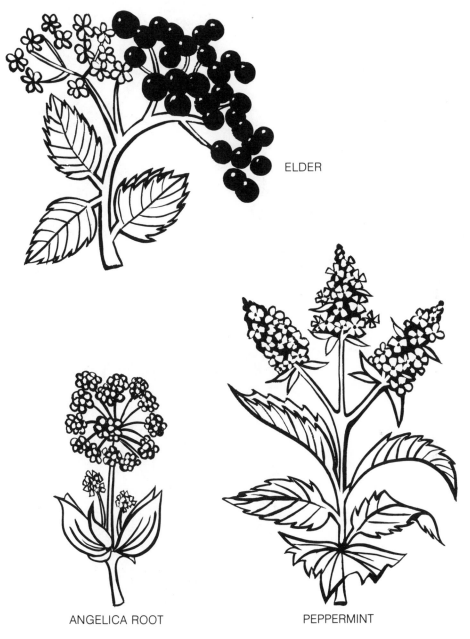

ELDER

ANGELICA ROOT   PEPPERMINT

Fig. 7–9. *Flowering herbs.*

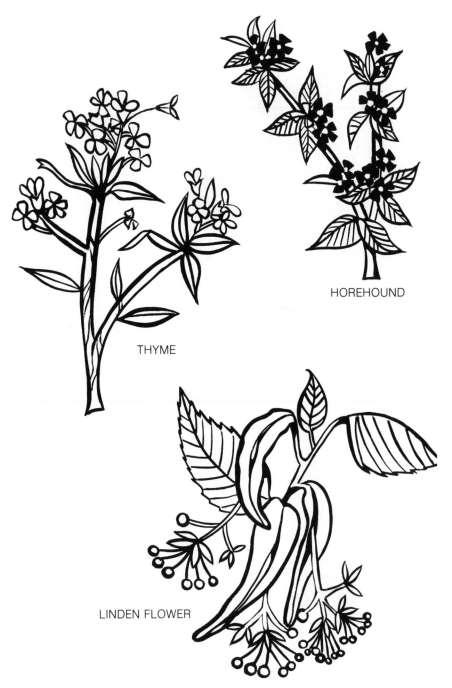

HOREHOUND

THYME

LINDEN FLOWER

Fig. 7–10. *Flowering herbs.*

8

Christmas Tree Ornaments

Folk art adds a touch of warmth and originality to the house, and Christmas tree ornaments have always been more than just decorations when they were handpainted. I have always regarded them as heirlooms to be handed down through the family. There are many types of hand-made ornaments, but the queen of them all is the handpainted piece. This chapter provides patterns for eight ornaments (see also color section), but do not stop with these. Let your imagination run wild, and you will think of many new designs for your tree.

The best wood for ornaments is Finland Birch, about $\frac{1}{8}$ to $\frac{3}{16}$ inch thick. A larger size might be too heavy for your tree branch. You will have to spend little time preparing Finland Birch because of its hard surface. Heavy cardboard or a composite material can be used, but wood is preferred because of its quality.

Trace the pattern from the book and transfer its outline with graphite paper to the wood. Cut out the shape with a jig saw or band saw, and drill a small hole at the center top of the design for a ribbon or fine chain to hang the ornament with. Sand any rough edges, clean, and apply a base coat with a water-based paint. Once the base coat has dried, you can paint your design over it.

Place the tracing of the pattern over the painted wooden cutout. Slip graphite paper, shiny side down, under the tracing and retrace over the design to transfer it to the wood. Then flip the tracing over (so it

Fig. 8–1. *Hand-painted Christmas tree ornaments are truly special.*

matches the shape of the wood) and transfer the pattern to the other side of the cutout.

Your design is now ready for painting. Use the colors suggested in the captions for the designs. You can use either the acrylic or the tole painting method. Use a #5 brush for larger areas, and a #2 brush for details. Allow one side to dry completely before painting the other. After decorative painting has dried thoroughly, the ornament may be antiqued with the mud stain (see chapter 5). Then coat the ornament with a low lustre varnish or polyurethane. Let it dry for 24 hours before hanging.

Fig. 8–2. *Standing angel. (1) ultramarine blue mixed with white; (2) Grumbacher red mixed with a little white; (3) white; (4) orange mixed with white.*

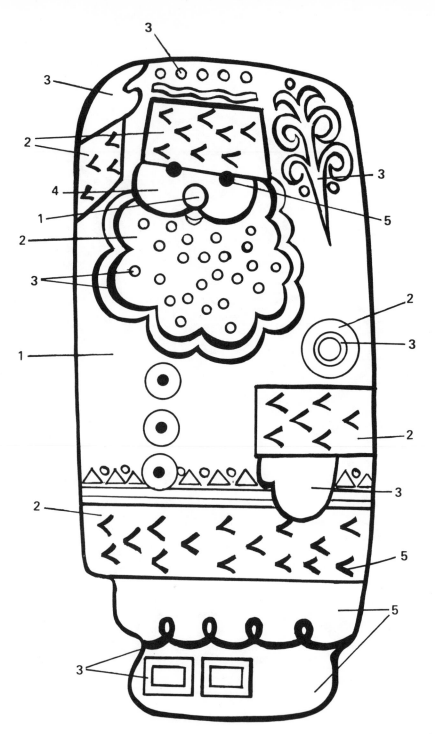

Fig. 8–3. *Santa Claus. (1) red mixed with white; (2) white; (3) yellow ochre; (4) white mixed with a little red; (5) black.*

[80]

Fig. 8–4. *Ice skate. (1) yellow ochre; (2) manganese or cerulean blue mixed with a little white; (3) Grumbacher red; areas shown in black, paint black.*

[81]

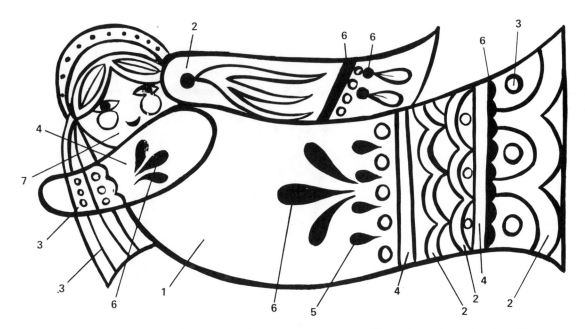

Fig. 8-5. *Angel.* (1) red: (2) turquoise; (3) yellow ochre; (4) pink; (5) white; (6) black; (7) flesh (white mixed with a very small amount of red, with slightly more red for cheeks).

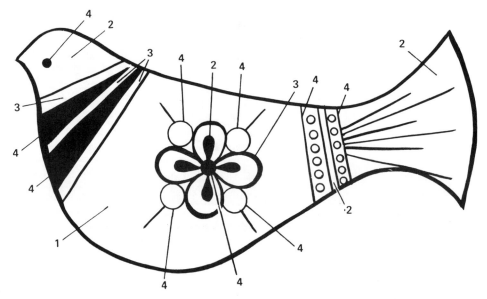

Fig. 8-6. *Dove.* (1) red mixed with white; (2) Grumbacher red; (3) permanent green light mixed with white and yellow ochre; (4) ultramarine blue mixed with a little white.

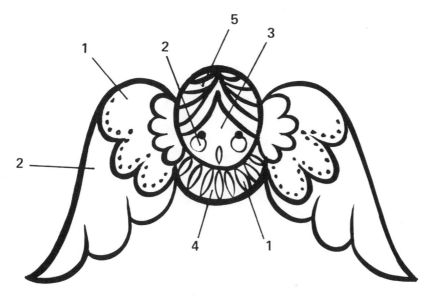

Fig. 8–7. *Winged angel. (1) turquoise; (2) pink; (3) white; (4) light green (white mixed with a little green and yellow ochre); (5) orange.*

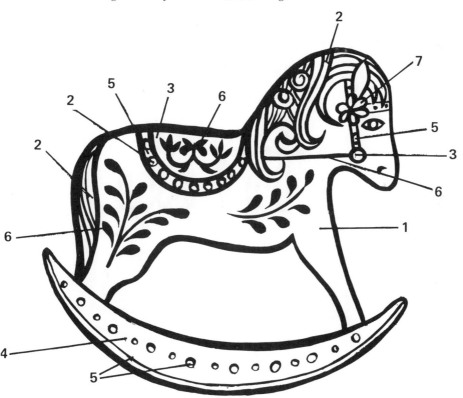

Fig. 8–8. *Rocking horse. (1) light blue; (2) yellow ochre and white; (3) pink; (4) lavender, (5) red; (6) deep blue (ultramarine blue, touch of red, touch of white); (7) white.*

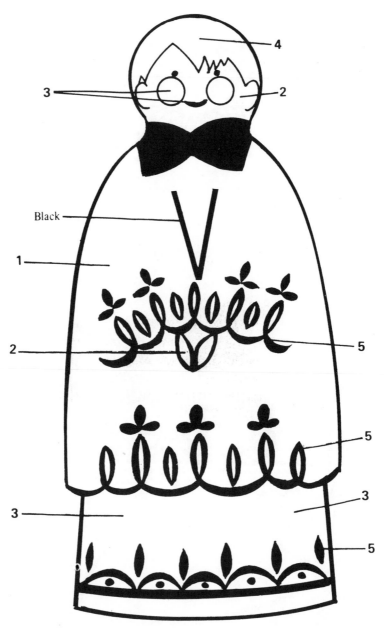

Fig. 8–9. *Choirboy. (1) white; (2) flesh (white mixed with a little red); (3) Grumbacher red; (4) orange mixed with a little white; (5) yellow ochre; areas shown in black, paint black.*

[84]

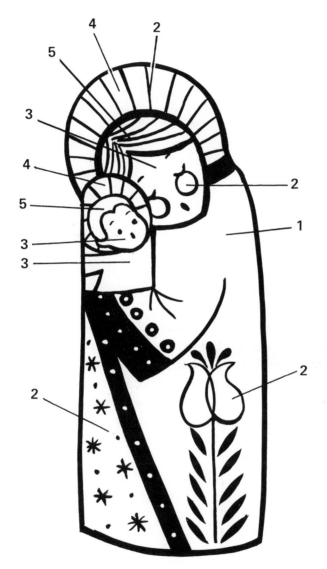

Fig. 8–10. *Madonna and child. (1) manganese or cerulean blue mixed with white; (2) red mixed with white; (3) flesh (white mixed with a little red); (4) permanent green light mixed with white; (5) orange mixed with white; areas shown in black, paint black.*

9

Restoring and Decorating a Trunk

Wooden trunks are high on the list for collectors, and they are becoming harder to find as the demand grows. With perseverance, however, you can locate the trunk of your choice. Hunt through antique shops, flea markets and garage sales. You might even find a forgotten trunk in a relative's attic.

Today trunks are used for just about everything. They enhance almost any room in the house, especially living rooms and bedrooms. In the living room, trunks make excellent coffee tables, storage bins for wood or magazines, or a place for the hooked rug that is being worked on. The bedroom could always use another place for sheets, blankets or clothing. Trunks also make fine night tables. A new bride would be delighted with a decorated trunk for her new linens. The list goes on and on.

Refinishing a wooden trunk is not as difficult as you might imagine. Before you begin, decide on the shape of the trunk. If a coffee table is what you want, look for a flat top. A barrel-shaped lid offers more room for storage. Check the condition thoroughly. Look for sturdy construction with hardware in fair condition. If one in good condition is not available, do not pass up one that can be salvaged. For instance, leather straps in poor shape can be removed or replaced; slats can be removed to make room for more art work, and broken hardware can be replaced.

Cleaning the trunk

Remove all handles, hinges, straps and locks. Use a claw hammer and pull at an angle, as often the nails are driven in at an angle for extra strength. Should any of the hardware be difficult to remove, do not force the nails or you will damage the wood. Leave the stubborn hardware on—it can be polished after the trunk is refinished.

Check the interior for peeling paint, torn linings, or worn paper. If its condition is good, a thorough cleaning will be sufficient. Remove peeling paint with varnish and paint remover. Prime with gesso when dry to fill the pores of the wood. The interior is ready for paint, stain or lining. If the trunk has a torn lining, remove it to allow musty odors to escape. A solution of wallpaper remover can be used. Again, gesso when ready. Working outdoors will make the task more pleasant and hasten the drying time.

Remove outside paint or finish with water-based paint remover. Apply with brush or rag and allow it to penetrate for several minutes, according to instructions on can. Wipe off with cloth, and then steel wool. Wear rubber gloves, as these paint removers can burn the skin. Work outdoors if possible; some removers have strong fumes. Take off excess remover with fine steel wool and denatured alcohol.

Preparing the wood

Carefully inspect for injuries to wood surface. Wood putty works best for filling in deep depressions or knot holes. To fill knot holes, first fold a piece of cardboard small enough to fit in hole. Using a knife, add putty a little at a time. Putty sometimes shrinks; therefore, work layers higher than the surface. Let all repairs dry thoroughly, and sand entire trunk even and smooth.

Most trunks have aged considerably; the wood is dry and needs replenishing. To treat the wood, heat in a double boiler one part raw linseed oil, two parts turpentine, and a small amount of Japan drier. Stir and simmer it a few minutes. Be careful, this mixture is highly flammable. Let the mixture cool to lukewarm or room temperature.

You are now ready to saturate the wood. Dip a clean cloth in the mixture and wipe it over the entire surface until the wood is shiny wet. Let dry and repeat procedure. Next take a clean cloth dampened with turpentine and wipe over the surface, and then wash wood with soapy cloth. Allow three to four days for drying. When thoroughly dry, sand smooth with fine steel wool. The wood is now back to its original state with the new oils.

Painting the trunk

The trunk is ready for painting. Prime or undercoat with gesso before painting, and sand lightly when primer is dry. Select color of finish paint. Water-based paints are simple to handle and work as well as oils. Choose a harmonizing color for trim.

A few examples of color combinations that work well together are a light green background with a light coral trim, red base with a yellow ochre or gold accent, or olive green background with red trim. Keep in mind that all colors will darken slightly when mudded. When working on a baby's trunk, a treasure for any new mother, white with a pale blue or pink accent is a delight; pale yellow with a white trim looks beautiful after mudding. For a child's room, use bold, vibrant colors, for example yellows and blues, to create warm and cool contrasts. Pastel colors create a soft mellow feeling—for example, pale rose used with grey green.

You may use a wood stain as background. Surface should be stripped of paint, sanded with 0000 steel wool, and sealed with clear sealer. Mix a small amount of the stain into wood putty to slightly darken any repairs, making them less noticeable after staining. Use an oil stain to maintain the truest wood color. Stir often when working with stain, and apply with soft cloth or brush. After stain has penetrated, wipe off excess with clean cloth. Apply second coat if darker shade is desired.

When selecting the design for trunk, be aware of the shape of the area where design is to be placed. The design should be planned to fill most of that space in an interesting way (see figures 9-1–9-3). A flying

Fig. 9–1. *Designs for a trunk should be planned to fit the space.*

Fig. 9–2.   Pennsylvania Dutch designs adapted to a trunk.

angel, horse or elongated arrangement of flowers and leaves works well in a rectangle. Designs of angels and flowers, or children's figures or animals lend themselves well to a child's trunk. A birthdate and name could be worked into the design. A design painted inside the lid is a surprise each time the trunk is opened.

A red background could feature fruits and flowers together. Yellow pears, pale green grapes, and white blossoms would be charming in any room. With a dark background, paint the pattern with light colors for contrast. A background of a light color should feature darker hues in the pattern. Use bright, clear hues, as the mud stain will mellow all the colors.

Trace design on tracing paper and place over the area where pattern will appear. Tape with masking tape in two upper corners. Slide graphite paper with shiny side face down under tracing and draw over

Fig. 9–3. *Two more ideas for decorating trunks.*

pattern to transfer to trunk. Paint design following the basic instructions given in earlier chapters.

Mud staining and varnishing

Once the art work is fully complete, you are ready to antique with the mud, as described in chapter 5. You will find it easier to work with than most commercial stains, as it is thicker and you have more control of lights and darks. Rub mud over surface of the wood with brush or cloth; wipe off with clean cloth until all excess has been removed. Lighten background color with small amount of linseed oil on clean cloth. Using a circular motion, rub off the mud to desired degree. Edges should remain darker than center for antique look. Use mud lightly to shade art work.

Once mud stain is dry, the trunk is ready for varnish. Do not use decoupage one-coat varnish, as it will not stand up to the use a trunk will get. I have found satin polyurethane to be the most durable. If you prefer to work with regular varnish, egg shell or low-lustre is best. Varnish with at least three coats, letting it dry thoroughly between coats, preferably for 24 hours. Sand between each coat with 0000 steel wool, using tack cloth to remove excess steel wool. After final coat, you may sand lightly and then wax with parquet wax. This last step is optional.

The lining

You have now arrived at the fun part. Selecting the color for the lining brings out the interior decorator in you. Choose a fabric (either plain or quilted) to suit the nature of the trunk. A provincial look is achieved with cotton calico, a patchwork print, or chintz. For a feminine or dainty appearance, use small printed florals, pastel stripes, velvet or solid pastels. For the more tailored look, fabric of a slightly heavier texture is used: burlap, sailcloth, felt, corduroy, ticking, and paisley prints. Wallpaper can be used, but a protective varnish covering is needed; paper is not as durable as fabric.

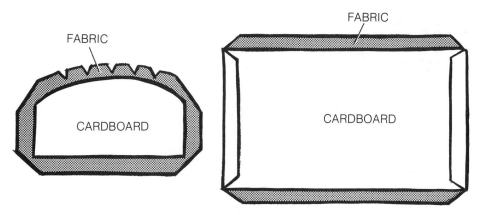

Fig. 9–4. *Left: shows cardboard on material for lid side. Clip corners and curves to eliminate bulky overlaps. Right: shows two sides of material folded over cardboard.*

Be sure lining color harmonizes with exterior color. Do not allow colors to fight each other. A pale pink trunk would work well with a deep cranberry tone inside, either printed or plain. A white trunk needs a strong color, such as red. If the art work is rather busy on the exterior, the lining should be quiet with less busy pattern.

Lining is done by covering thin cardboard pattern pieces with fabric and then gluing these pieces into place. Cut the cardboard slightly smaller than actual inside dimensions to allow for fabric and cardboard thickness at joints. A thin padding may be placed between the fabric and cardboard; cut it ⅛ inch smaller than the cardboard. The lining material should overlap the cardboard at least 1 inch on all sides. Cut the corners and any curved edges as shown on left of figure 9-4 to eliminate bulky overlaps. Turn the fabric under and glue to the cardboard. Use white glue so the fabric can be pulled off if sizing errors are made.

Glue the covered cardboard to the trunk, doing sides first, then front and back, and then the bottom. The lid should be done in the same manner. Braiding or ribbon may be glued or fastened with upholstery tacks along the edges for a decorative touch.

10

Tavern Signs

Tavern signs, with their wide variety of artistic shapes, have great appeal to the inventive decorator. Today there are many uses for attractively decorated signs. Creating your own house sign offers many satisfactions. A sign with a favorite recipe would bring charm to any kitchen. A combination sign and mirror for the bathroom would be a unique touch. A sign with animals, boats, figures, or trains in a child's room would be cherished long after childhood. A handlettered sign for a shopkeeper friend would make a lasting gift.

Colonial tavern signs were widely used in the eighteenth century (figure 10-1). A walk down the main street of a typical eighteenth century town in England would take you past signs for the chemist, the ship's merchant, the grain dealer, the hatter, the cabinetmaker, the tanner, the barber, the shoemaker, the apothecary, and of course the tavern keeper. Signs with symbols were necessary for tradesmen to attract the public. Symbols and pictures were commonly used for communication, since many people could not read or write. Subjects for signboards varied greatly and included landscapes, decorative symbols, animals, portraits, and the ever-present eagle. Signs were used not only to indicate retail shops, services and taverns, but also to designate houses and to post rates at toll roads and bridges. Many of these grand old signs are in private collections and museums today.

Figures 10-2 and 10-3 offers several designs and shapes for your

Fig. 10–1. *Tavern signs are an ever-popular tole project.*

own indoor, outdoor signboard. But don't limit yourself to these; you'll discover many more possibilities. Wood signs can be cut from pine, plywood, paperboard, or several composites found on the market today.

Signboards can be painted using either the acrylic or tole method. Embellish your signs with touches of flowers, squiggles, and striping motifs. It all adds up to a sure sign of your creativity.

[95]

Fig. 10–2. *Typical colonial tavern signs.*

Fig. 10–3. *Ideas for your "colonial" shingles or tavern signs.*

11

Hex Signs

Traditionally Pennsylvania Dutch barns were painted red with wooden ornamental decorations on the outer walls at a considerable height from the ground. The purpose of these hex signs was to protect the barn from lightning and the livestock from the work of witches. Today many barns with these symbols have been painted over, proving that the superstition no longer prevails.

The huge signs were laid out with a large wooden compass. They were often 4 to 6 feet in diameter and were arranged in balanced areas across the barn. Fresh, bold colors were used—yellow, green, red and blue, with white accents. Petals and stars were arranged in large circular shapes. Scalloped edges and bold colors bordered the sign. The contrast against the red of the barn was very attractive. Today decorated barns, while not as prevalent as in the past, may still be seen in Lehigh, Montgomery and Bucks counties, Pennsylvania.

Although you may never decorate a barn, hex signs like those in figures 11-1, 11-2, and 11-3 can be included in many folk art designs on much smaller objects. Bold color combinations are an important part of these geometric designs, and suggested color schemes are given for two of the signs (figures 11-2 and 11-3).

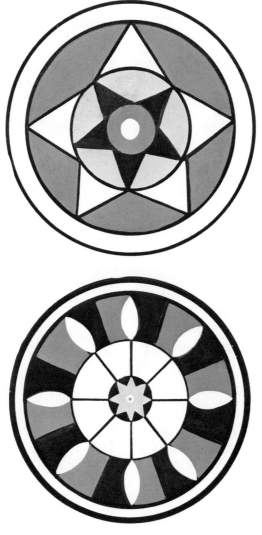

Fig. 11–1. *Typical hex designs.*

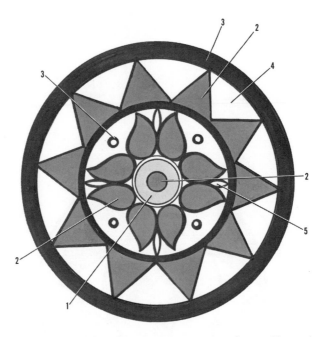

Fig. 11–2. *Hex sign with tulips.* (1) *green;* (2) *red;* (3) *blue;* (4) *yellow;* (5) *white.*

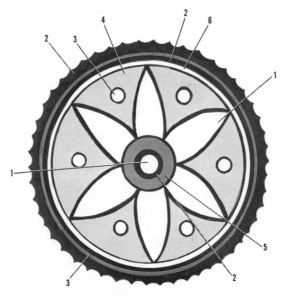

Fig. 11–3. *Scalloped edge hex sign.* (1) *yellow;* (2) *red;* (3) *green;* (4) *light blue;* (5) *blue;* (6) *white.*

〔 100 〕

12

Mirrors

Mirrors in the home have always been a useful and decorative item. As seen in the accompanying figures, mirrors come in a wide variety of shapes: Federal or Empire; a simple square with plain molding; ovals; ornamental mirrors with fluted edges; rectangular, horizontal, or full length mirrors; mirrors set in clocks; mirrors used in conjunction with paintings; sconces with mirrors set in center; long rectangular shelves with a mirror for a backboard. There are mirrors for every room in the house. Why not design and make your own? Here is the chance to be very practical and creative.

Design the shape of the frame you want to make, and refer back to chapter 2 for instructions on cutting your own wood piece. Then review the instructions in chapter 2 for preparing a new wood surface. Paint the base coat, using two coats of low-lustre acrylic or latex paint. When the base coat is dry, transfer your design to the frame (see chapter 3). Paint the design with acrylics for a smoother, more durable finish, and mud stain if desired.

Use a clean bristle brush to apply two coats of a satin varnish; dry thoroughly between coats. After the second coat has dried, rub it with 0000 steel wool. This will remove any imperfections from the varnish. Use a tack cloth to wipe the mirror before varnishing again. Four coats are sufficient; use the 0000 steel wool after the third and fourth coats.

Use the technique of wet sanding to make the frame feel like

CONSTITUTIONAL

QUEEN
ANNE

PENNSYLVANIA
DUTCH

Fig. 12–1. *Historical styles of mirror frames.*

EMPIRE

VENETIAN

MASSACHUSETTS

COUNTRY FRENCH

Fig. 12–2. *Historical styles of mirror frames.*

NEW
ENGLAND

VICTORIAN

Fig. 12–3.   *Historical styles of mirror frames.*

Fig. 12–4. *A mirror frame covered with "untraditional" field flowers and grasses still has a folk art look.*

porcelain. Dip the finest grain sandpaper into a soapy water solution. Make the solution with tepid water and a few drops of detergent, and swish the sandpaper in it until it is wetted down. Using light circular motions, rub the entire frame; its surface will appear milky white. Rinse it quickly and dry thoroughly. When dry, rub a parquet wax (sold in craft stores) over the surface. Buff lightly when dry, and our frame is ready for a mirror. Have the mirror cut to size, and attach it to the back of the frame with molding strips.

13

Portrait Painting

Folk art is not limited to painting designs of fruits, flowers, and birds. It is most rewarding to paint a portrait in the folk art style on wood or canvas.

For beginners

The beginner will find it easier to simplify features and clothing until colors become familiar, and drawing feels comfortable and natural. Practice drawing friends and members of your family to achieve a better knowledge of proportions. Trace over several portraits in this chapter to experience the shapes of faces.

Painting on wood is interesting for the primitive look it creates. Canvas should be used to adjust to the flexibility and nature of painting on a non-rigid surface.

Acrylic paints mean easier clean-up and color mixing for the beginner because they are water soluble. Acrylics may be used thick or thin for a varied effect. Review chapter 5 to refresh your knowledge of working with acrylics.

Color mixing is very important to the beginner. Shading and highlighting should be kept to a minimum. The key elements to learn

[107]

first are drawing and color mixing. Simple warm and cool color combinations will quickly teach the student about color theory.

Color combinations between background and clothing are crucial to every portrait. If the background is a warm hue, such as a dark red, the clothing should be a complement like a light green or cool blue or turquoise. When in doubt about a color combination, remember a primary color is toned or greyed down by the use of its complement, and secondary colors are made by mixing two primary colors. Skin should always be the lightest hue in a portrait. Highlights illuminate the face, making it the focal point of the painting. Use white with red and yellow ochre as the basic skin color.

Composition is a blueprint for your painting. If the proportions and shapes are not correct, the portrait will fail. Study the proportions of the face and measure distances from the top of head to the eyes, from eyes to nose, nose to lips, and from lips to chin (figure 13-1). You need to know these distances, but as you become more proficient, you won't have to measure them.

Practice head proportions by copying figure 13-1. Start with an egg shape the same size your portrait will be. Draw a horizontal line through the center of the head. The eyes lie in the middle of the head's length. The face is then divided into thirds. Halfway between the eyes and chin is the base of nose, and halfway between the end of nose and chin is the center of lips. Once you locate the basic features, begin filling them in. Place pupils in the centers of eyes, eyebrows above the eyes, and complete the nose. Complete the lips by drawing the corners of the mouth directly under each eye. Shoulders should extend slightly beyond neck for a young girl. Figure 13-2 shows the finished drawing.

Practice color recipes for skin, cheeks, lips and hair. When choosing clothing colors, keep in mind the warm and cool theory of color mixing in chapter 4. The color section shows the finished portrait.

For advanced painters

Decide the style of the portrait you will paint. Is it a primitive portrait, or a realistic traditional style? Since this is a folk art book, I

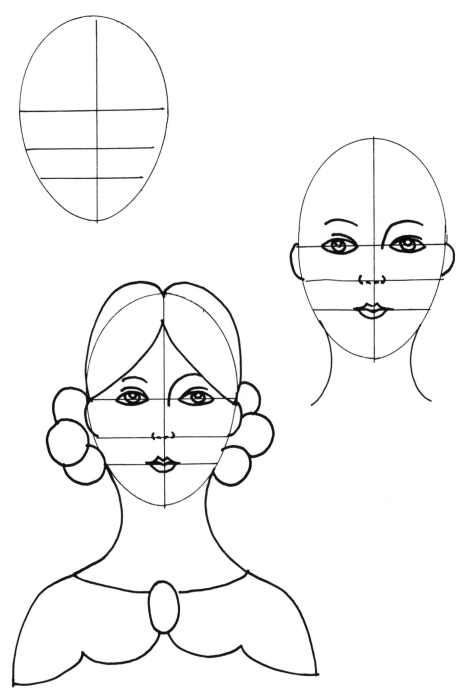

Fig. 13-1. *Proportions of the head.*

Fig. *13–2.* *Finished sketch, begun in figure 13–1.*

would like to stay with the primitive style of painting. Figures 13-3 through 13-7 provide examples of "portraits" for you to copy and paint. Colors for the primitive style are muted tones rather than bold, vibrant hues. The old world look is what you should strive for.

Be aware of placement of the subject on your canvas. A head placed too low will give the illusion of falling or sliding off the board. Place the head a quarter of the way down from the top for balance.

When your drawing is complete, decide what combinations of

Fig. 13–3. *Colonial gentleman.*

Fig. 13–4. *Formal portrait of a child.*

color to use. The background should be toned down and shaded to add depth to the painting.

All hair colors are basically versions of yellow to which several colors have been added. Brunette hair has shadings of yellow green to which burnt sienna and ultramarine blue have been added. Highlights are grey violet with white added. Blonde hair has shadings with a mix-

Fig. 13–5.   *Young man.*

Fig. 13–6. *Young lady.*

[114]

Fig. 13–7. *Woman in formal pose.*

ture of thalo crimson, ultramarine blue, white and yellow. Highlight with yellow green plus white.

For the basic skin tone, always use white as a base, adding yellow ochre and red. Do not start with skin too light. A middle value is placed first, then shaded using a touch of green or blue in the flesh tone. Highlight is yellow ochre and white with a touch of red.

When you paint clothing, keep in mind the value and strength of its color in relation to the face. The face is the main feature of the portrait; the clothing is secondary and should not overpower the face. Clothing and background colors should complement and enhance the face. For example, a dark green dress will complement a muted red. Two cool colors could work together as long as a warmer hue is introduced with them. A middle muted green background with light blue dress, for instance, will work if red hair or a red hat is added to complement the cool colors.

Starting with the background, paint from the upper left corner across the portrait. Paint the background around the model's head. With a clean brush, paint the skin tone starting with the forehead. Paint the middle skin value first, then the shadows, and finish the skin with highlighting. Always work from the top down.

In figure 13-8, the entire facial area is painted with a middle value skin tone. The eyes and mouth are then blocked in with dark tones, and the shape of the hair is filled in with the hair tone. Next, the flesh tone is mixed with small amounts of green, ultramarine blue and burnt sienna for the shading tone. Shadows are painted over the eyes and down the sides of the nose (darker on right side).

In figure 13-9, the hat is painted in a light off-white blue mixed from white, blue, yellow ochre and a touch of red. The lighter flesh tones are then worked in over the forehead, down the nose, and on the chin and cheeks.

The background should be darker behind the highlighted side of the face to accentuate it. Add the rest of the background as you work down. Fill in the light and dark areas of the clothing. Do not add details until all colors have been established. When you feel the portrait is balanced for color, come back and work in the details. Never overwork a painting with too much detail—it will look artificial.

Fig. 13–8. *Basic skin and hair tones are painted first, then shading begins to fill out features.*

Fig. 13–9. *The hat is shaped in around the hair, and highlights are added to the face.*

Fig. *13–10. Details are added and final shading and highlights.*

In figure 13-10, the details of the hat, earring and clothing have been added after the final facial tones were highlighted and smoothed. Note the small white highlights on the end of the nose, in the pupils, and on the earring. This portrait can also be seen in the color section.

Glazing

Glazing brings out the truly exciting characteristics of acrylics in portrait painting. Glazing refers to a transparent wash of color being brushed over dried colors. Thinned tones painted over each other create colors that appear to have dimension.

Glazes must be applied with great care. The brush must be free from all particles and cleaned well. Place a puddle of water on the palette. Mix a small amount of acrylic medium with water and a touch of a color used in shading, such as green, blue, or burnt sienna. Never use white in glazing, as it is opaque and the transparency is lost when mixed with glazes. Mix the water and colors until transparent on palette. With a clean brush wash over shaded area and let dry. For a richer tone, apply a second glaze. This method can be applied to clothing and background shadings. For lighter areas needing a rich tone, mix yellow ochre and Grumbacher red with water and medium. Apply over areas and let dry.

Glazing the shadows and highlights of hair creates a luminous effect. Glazing skin tones causes richer tones with visible depth. Use glazes often and practice applying the proper depth of color on white paper. Too much white paper showing through the wash indicates that not enough pigment was used.

When portrait is complete, you can varnish it with either acrylic varnish spray or acrylic medium.

14

Painting on Fabric

Fabric painting is only one of many new methods of painting with acrylics. Boutiques and art galleries are searching for handpainted objects other than paintings on canvas. The versatility and permanence of acrylics make them a fine medium for painting on materials other than canvas, wood or metal.

You might consider these few ideas for fabric painting:

Wall hangings with oversized flowers and leaves in springtime colors.

Bell pulls with center designs of elaborate birds, flowers and intricate scrolls resembling those of the early French in New York (figure 14-1). It could hang next to the fireplace or a bookcase for a colonial look.

Kites made of a fine cotton batiste, with a painting of a lovely bird. Flying high in the wind, it would bring joy to any child.

Youngster's sneakers covered with hearts and flowers.

Aprons for children and grownups—these are always useful.

Tablecloths with landscapes painted from favorite photographs (figure 14-2).

Gaily decorated evening clothes, with a matching design on an evening bag (figure 14-3).

[121]

Fig. 14-1. *Design ideas for bell pulls.*

Fig. 14–2. *Tablecloth with landscape.*

Denim for sports jacket, jeans, vest or skirt, featuring signs of the
zodiac, floral patterns, or other folk art or contemporary designs
(figure 14-4).

Children's clothing with nursery rhyme characters, cartoons, animals, or dolls (figures 14-5 and 14-6).

Curtains, window shades, room screens (figure 14-7), drapes, and
bedspreads.

[123]

Fig. 14–3. *Personalize an evening dress with a folk design.*

Fig. 14–4. *Jeans can be decorated with flowers or favorite pictures.*

All-cotton fabrics should be used. Synthetics do not absorb paints into the fibers, which is needed for durability during repeated washings. Material can be as heavy as burlap or as shear as batiste. Painted fabrics can be put in washing machines and dryers. The paint is good for many years of wear.

[125]

Assemble the following basic materials before starting:

Acrylic paints, same color selection as in chapter 4
Brushes—short-handled, pointed red sable #5 and #2
Fabric or clothing to be painted
Old album cover or cardboard
Gesso, to be used on heavy fabrics such as denim
Tracing paper
Dressmaker transfer paper in variety of colors
Masking tape
Straight pins
Vinegar

Step 1: Wash all new fabrics before applying paint to remove sizing, allowing the fibers to become porous. Iron the fabric before applying paint.

Step 2: Trace your selected design using tracing paper. Transfer the pattern to the fabric by using dressmaker's carbon paper under the tracing. Place the album cover or cardboard under the area that will be painted, stretching the fabric slightly. Tack the fabric to the board with straight pins at top and bottom. For jeans, cut the cardboard to fit the working area of the leg. On heavy fabric such as denim, paint a light coat of gesso inside the design shape. This will prevent wear on a high-quality brush and require less paint. Gesso dries in ten minutes, and the design is ready to paint. Several thin coats of paint are best, and the paint should soak into the fabric. Do not allow the paint to become too thick on the fabric.

Step 3: Allow the paint to dry thoroughly. Place fabric on an ironing board, and saturate a clean cloth with equal parts of vinegar and water and squeeze out the excess. Place the cloth over the garment and iron with dry iron to set the paint in the fibers.

Fig. 14–5. *Nursery characters are good designs for children's items.*

Fig. 14–6. *Stylized animals dress up children's clothes.*

Fig. 14–7. *Painted fabric can be put to striking use on a room divider.*

15

Troubleshooting: Questions and Answers

Through the years of teaching, I have become aware of questions that always arise. I would like to share a few of the questions with their answers so that they can be helpful to you.

Question: After several weeks of painting, my brush loses its point and the bristles separate. Could it be that there is paint in the brush even though I wash it each and every time it is used?

Answer: Yes. Acrylic paint must be washed out thoroughly after every color is used. A build-up of paint occurs rapidly because acrylic is a plastic paint. When the paint collects in the neck of the brush, the bristles will separate. Every two or three weeks, clean with Aquatec cleaner, Craftint acrylic remover, or nailpolish remover. Pour a small amount in a saucer and swish the brush several times in it to loosen the paint. Wipe with a clean cloth. Repeat several times until the cloth shows no sign of paint. It is surprising how much paint can be removed from a brush that looks clean to the eye. Wash brush with soap and water after using cleaning solution.

Question: When working on a wooden plaque, I find that after the piece has been painted with water-based paint, the wood feels rough to the touch although I sanded before painting.

Answer: When water-based paint is used, a light sanding with

0000 steel wool between coats is needed. Two coats of base paint are all that is required. Water-based paint lifts the grain of the wood, causing your problem.

Question: When painting my art work on a metal piece previously painted with high-gloss paint, the art work rubs off very easily. Should I apply the paint thicker for the art work?

Answer: Do not use high-gloss paint for metal. The finish creates problems because it is hard for the acrylic to adhere to such a surface. Satin or flat paint will be much easier to work with. Keeping the acrylic creamy and not too thin will help prevent it from rubbing off easily. There is now a new metal primer that has a water base. Once applied, you can use water-based finish coat; in the past only oil paint could be used over oil primer.

Question: I find with acrylic paint when I try to achieve a flat opaque texture, I get ridges and a thickness I cannot undo. Is the paint too thick?

Answer: There is a possibility that you may be using too small a brush. Too many strokes create ridges. Always use the larger brush for background or flat areas. If paint is too thick, add a few drops of water to thin.

Question: What can I use to thin down the mud? After many uses, I find it dries and is not as manageable.

Answer: Use a little linseed oil, and stir well. Turpentine will make it very runny and it will not adhere the way it should. Never apply the mud too thickly on a surface. It creates more work for you to remove it, and it is wasted. A little goes a long way.

Question: When painting fruit, I find that I cannot achieve a bright enough highlight.

Answer: There can be several reasons for this. The basic color of the fruit may not be dark enough for contrast. If it is light, and the highlight is light, the difference cannot be seen. Experiment until you find the correct value. Another reason could be that the highlight may need a touch of the complementary color added to the white. When mixing a highlight with the complement, start with white and add only a slight amount of the color. Often in folk art, white alone is sufficient, but if a more realistic look is desired, follow the above.

Question: I have completed a wood piece which I am very pleased with, except for the distress marks. Mine are going in several directions, and the result is a busy appearance.

Answer: Never overwork the distress marks. Always go with the grain of the wood. What you are trying to achieve is a split or cracked look, or a worn feeling to the item. A screwdriver or small file can create suitable effects. File the edge of work in various places, but do not overwork it. This will give the worn look to the edges, and when mudded gives it quite an antique feeling.

Question: The end result of most of my wood pieces is too dark. The original color can barely be seen. Am I leaving too much mud on the surface?

Answer: Yes. When removing the mud with linseed oil, be sure to use clean cloth constantly, otherwise you will be putting back the mud you removed. Always work in circular motions when removing mud, and do a small area at a time.

Question: What is the difference between thalo colors and regular colors?

Answer: Thalo colors produce a true and permanent color. They have the highest degree of intensity when mixed with white. Thalo colors are transparent and are excellent for glazing and washes. They become beautifully opaque when mixed with white.

Question: I recently painted a tablecloth with acrylic paint. I attempted this on my own since I could not find instructions on how to do it. After washing, my art work cracked slightly. What did I do wrong?

Answer: Be sure to thin paint considerably with water, as paint has to be worked into fabric with brush several times to penetrate. Once acrylic has worked itself into fabric, it is there permanently, and will not wash out or crack. What may have happened to yours was that your paint was too thick to seep into fibers. Article may be washed in washing machine and dried in automatic dryer.

16

Motifs and
Patterns

The decorative possibilities of folk and tole painting are innumerable. From hand mirrors to furniture, toys to portraits, each object presents a special challenge to come up with the perfect design to paint on it. We all would like to be designers, but even the best designers need sources. On the pages that follow you will find over 50 original folk art and tole motifs and patterns that you can use any way you want. Trace and enlarge them, use parts of several to compose a new combination, or use them as inspiration for creating your own designs. Then get out your paints and brushes and have fun!

BORDERS

[145]

[148]

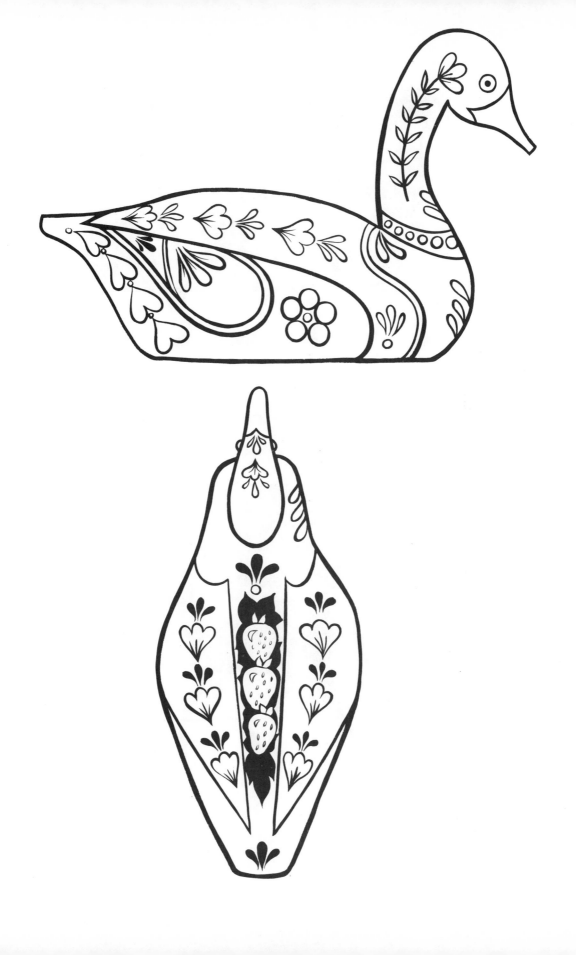

[161]

{ 163 }